THE SLAVE SHIP

(Original Title: The Long Black Schooner)

Emma Gelders Sterne

Illustrated by David Lockhart

AN
APPLE
PAPERBACK

SCHOLASTIC INC.
New York Toronto London Auckland Sydney

ISBN 0-590-40621-3

12 11 10 9 8 7 6 5 4 3 2 1   1   8 9/8 0 1 2 3/9

Printed in the U.S.A.   11

Contents

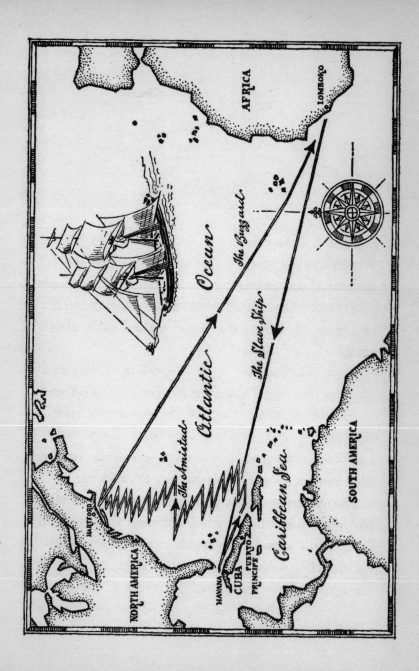

1. The Barracoon

WE will have our coffee under the trees if that pleases you, señores." The governor of the island of Cuba rose from dinner and led his four guests into the soft night. The dinner had lasted for two hours. It was good to stand up and move about again.

When they reached the door leading to the patio, the governor stood aside for his guests to go ahead of him. First, Nicholas Trist, the American consul; then the two planters from the south end of the island, Pedro Montez and young Pepé Ruiz; finally, the stranger, a Yankee sea captain, Ezra Stone.

The governor was a good host, and the evening had gone well on the whole; though the stranger, the Yankee seaman, had made conversation a little difficult. The other American, Mr. Trist, was almost like a Cuban. He had lived for years in the island and spoke excellent Spanish. His ideas, too, and his tastes were like those of the governor and of Montez and Ruiz, the sugar planters.

Señor Montez and the gay young Pepé were strangers to the governor only because they lived several days' journey down the island, at Puerto Principe. After the first half-hour at his table, he did not hesitate to think of them as his friends. It was the sea captain from the States who had kept his host on edge during the dinner. Trist had warned that Captain Stone had peculiar ideas about slavery.

Armed with this knowledge, the governor had succeeded in keeping the conversation away from this subject. But it had not been easy, since Montez and Ruiz had come up to Havana for the express purpose of buying newly arrived Africans.

By the time dessert had been served, the governor was glad of a change of scene, so he had suggested having coffee in the garden. The view of the harbor and the distant lights of the city always served to start a pleasant flow of conversation. He busied himself directing the servants, who brought easy chairs and lanterns to the patio and moved about serving the coffee with practiced skill.

But Captain Stone did not seat himself in the

chair provided for his comfort. He wandered about restlessly, looking out at the night.

"You'll get a better view of our harbor from this side, señor," the governor said.

"Truly," agreed Ruiz. "The walls of the barracoon hide the water front on the east."

"Barracoon?" The Yankee captain was puzzled. It was not a word familiar to him in his small knowledge of Spanish.

"The slavepen, where they keep the slaves and ready them for market," Ruiz explained politely. He turned to his host. "The placing of the barracoon so near your country palace surprised me," he said. "But I suppose it was necessary to have a safe spot for unloading the ships from Africa. . . . What is a harbor for, if not to receive useful imports from over the world!"

Señor Montez chuckled. He was amused because he knew the real reason the governor kept the unsightly walls of the slavepens under his eye. The head of the Cuban government collected a certain amount of money for every slave brought into Havana. Now that importing Africans was no longer lawful, it was whispered that the governor's collections had doubled. In the years since the agreement with England was signed, forbidding the slave trade, the governor must have made a pretty penny.

Such things amused the planter. His small eyes were set close together like a pig's eyes. But they had wrinkles around them from laughter. He laughed often, but not pleasantly.

It amused him now to think of the governor sitting in his wonderful palace garden and watching the dark, forbidding walls of the slavepen. The walls cut off the view, but the business of buying and selling within the barracoon provided the governor with the money to pay for all this beauty.

Ezra Stone did not share Montez' knowledge. If he had, he would have seen nothing to laugh at. He saw no good in slavery. In his own country, the bringing of kidnaped Africans had, for twenty years, been forbidden under the Constitution. Now England had made a treaty with Spain and other European governments that their ships would no longer carry on the slave trade.

Captain Stone looked forward to the day when labor in the islands of the West Indies and on the plantations in the southern states of the United States would be carried on by free men, as it was in his own Connecticut.

"You'll soon have the harbor view free and clear,

I reckon," he said cheerfully. "With the slave trade stopped by the treaty, buying and selling of human beings will die out."

"My dear sir," the coffee cup shook in Nicholas Trist's hand as his anger rose. "My dear Captain Stone," he sputtered, "you are forgetting freedom of the seas! You can't take away a man's right to trade as he pleases by signing names on a treaty! You, sir, make your profits bringing clocks and silver pitchers from Connecticut. You take back sugar. The slave ships make their profits by bringing in Africans. A treaty will never stop them."

"You deal in sugar?" Ruiz asked, without giving the American seaman a chance to reply. "You make your living out of it? The sugar cane does not plant and cut itself, señor. My uncle, for instance, and my friend, Pedro Montez, are owners of great plantations. Less than half their money is in the land, the rest is spent in buying slaves to work the land. I am here to buy slaves for my uncle. Why? So that you may buy sugar!"

Ruiz turned to the governor. "I think I am informed correctly that a shipload of Africans arrived less than two weeks ago?"

The governor nodded. It was unfortunate that

the subject had come up. But there was no need to deny the facts.

"Freedom of the seas!" Ezra Stone answered. "What about freedom of the people who are kidnaped from their homes? This is not the Dark Ages. This is the year 1839."

The American consul, Nicholas Trist, sighed. He had heard such wild talk from some of his countrymen before. He had often silenced them with the simple reminder that the Africans were really fortunate to find a home in civilized countries. But tonight he did not want to continue the conversation longer than needful.

"I am a sincere friend of the Negroes," he said. "The only objection I can see to the slave trade is in the crowding of the ships which bring them across the water. The *Tecora*, the slaver that came in a few days ago, is an example of waste. Of the hundred taken on board in Africa, I am told that scarcely half lived to complete the journey. If the trade were more open and free, there would be no need to pack the cargo so tightly. Then the Negroes would not die."

Pedro Montez had scarcely listened to this idle talk. He had a question of his own. "Do you never have trouble—with the slavepens so close?"

The governor shook his head. "Never fear! The walls are high and strong, and the slaves are chained." Then he remembered his duties as host. He turned to Captain Stone. "I am afraid, señor, your coffee is cold."

The captain set down his cup. He must, he said, be going. His ship was sailing at dawn. . . .

"It was a mistake, my bringing the man to meet you," Nicholas Trist exclaimed when the Yankee was out of earshot. "But I thought, having a ship about to sail, he might be useful. I didn't know he'd been reading abolitionist stuff." Trist stirred his coffee angrily. "There's been too much of that. The abolitionists don't know what they are talking about! It's only in the places up North, where they know nothing of slavery, that they rail against it."

Trist continued to talk idly, in order to smooth over the memory of his countryman's rude remarks. "If it were not for the English law court and the English ships," he said, "the slave traffic could be carried on in perfect safety. Even so, I have been able to send many thousands of Africans to the States this year. I simply apply for shipping papers in the name of Ladinos, the name you give slaves who were in Cuba before the treaty. No one asks if they are Bozals, as you Cubans call the slaves lately out of Africa."

"Ladinos, of course." Ruiz stored the word in his mind, in case he had to ask for passports for the Bozals he intended buying on the morrow.

It was time to take leave of the governor. The evening had been pleasant after all, and not without profit. The planters had received some useful information. Their host clapped his hands. When a servant appeared, he ordered his carriage. "It is entirely safe to walk past the slavepens," he said. "But driving back to town will be pleasanter."

"Quicker, too," agreed Montez gratefully. He was anxious to get a good night's sleep. Tomorrow would be a busy day.

Ka-le woke. When he opened his eyes, he saw that dawn had not yet come. The light in the sky was still a smoky gray. The sun had not risen. But the boy had the feeling that his mother had wakened him, that she had called his name.

This in itself was strange, because of all the family Ka-le was always the first to wake up in the morning. The first ray of the rising sun that entered the doorway of the sleeping house was always the signal for him to leave his pallet.

Young boys were by habit and tradition the first to wake up in the village. As soon as the round ball of the sun was visible, Ka-le and his friends would leave the silent sleeping houses and go tumbling, prancing, running, down to the riverbank. They would throw off their loin cloths and bathe in the river. They prided themselves on getting up before the grownups.

Yet now, in the gray half-light before dawn, Ka-le was sure he had heard his mother calling. He must be mistaken, for his mother and sisters always slept until the sun was over the treetops.

He was about to close his eyes, turn over, and finish his sleep out when he heard the voice again —not close by, but at a distance: "Ka-le, my son, my son!" It was a cry of distress. The boy, still half asleep, leaped up to run toward the mournful voice. But at the first step, he stumbled and fell. Chains, bound to ankles, were not meant for running!

Wide awake now, bitterly awake, the boy pulled himself to his knees. How, even in his sleep, could he have forgotten? He was not safe in his village home, but a world away, across the dreadful ocean, and in chains!

He stared around the slavepen. The earth within the enclosure was brown and bare of trees. Along the high wall, overhanging roofs made a kind of lean-to. The lean-tos were like the sheds for cattle in the corral in the center of his village at home. But this was a corral for men, not for cattle.

For men? Women and girls, too, lay huddled on the ground within the high prison walls. His mother's voice had not been heard in a dream. She was here, in the slavepen, across the bare space under the shed with the other women and girls— his mother!

Ka-le pulled himself upright and started across the yard. He walked slowly, measuring his step by the length of the heavy chain fastened to iron bands on his ankles. He made his way past the sleeping forms and thought again how the slavepen resembled a corral for cattle.

But the cattle in his village were not chained. They wandered free in the meadows all day and were driven into the shelter of the corral only at night. The corral kept them safe from leopards and tigers who might stray down from the forests under cover of dark.

When he came up from his morning swim, Ka-le had always helped his father and the other men from the village lead the cattle to the grazing grounds.

Coming back from the fields, they would look for a sign, an omen, of what the day would bring. Sometimes they'd see a bright lizard or a bird with watchful eyes on its nest, or a misshapen twig, or a cloud that had a curious shape. Each thing had its own meaning. If the boys and men could not guess for themselves what the omen foretold, they would stop at the "palaver tree."

Here, seated on the platform of canework, under the great tree at the gate of the village, they'd find the old men. The elders would have come from their homes and would be found sitting under the tree, ready to greet strangers or settle arguments. The old men always had an answer. Long years had given the elders experience in every kind of sign or omen.

Ka-le looked down at his chains. He would never believe in omens again—not since the day when he had been seized with his mother and sold to the white men as slaves.

That day had been declared one of good omen. It had been the day of his sister's marriage. After the ceremonies, the whole family had gone beyond the village along the riverbank. They had gone to see the young couple start on their journey to the husband's home, in a neighboring village.

Ka-le's younger sisters had stopped on the river-bank to bathe with their friends in the sun-brightened water. His father had hurried home to see to his new cattle—the three new cows and a bull that had been the "bride's present" from the family of the groom. But Ka-le and his mother had climbed a little hill to catch a last glimpse of the voyagers' canoe.

The slave catchers must have been prowling in the underbrush, ready to snatch anyone who strayed too far from the safety of the village. The invaders had reached from the bushes and bound them with ropes and stuffed their mouths.

Ka-le's slow progress across the yard of the barracoon brought him close enough to the women's shelter to see his mother's garment of blue grasscloth. What was left of the tattered robe was pulled close about her body and over her face. The boy saw that she was still asleep. She must have called out his name in her sleep, as she had so many times on the slave ship.

They had not been chained to the same bench in the hold of the ship. Only by calling out to each other could they know that each still lived, where so many had died.

The boy bent down and smoothed the torn dress.

He remembered how carefully his mother had woven the cloth to wear to the wedding, and dyed the robe in the pot of indigo leaves. Now the garment was stained and torn, torn in the struggle with the kidnapers. It was stained with blood from wounds made by the leather thongs bound around her neck when she was captured. And this kidnaping had taken place on a day of good omen!

"No," Ka-le said aloud, as he turned back toward the place where the men and boys slept, "I will never believe in omens again!"

A man's voice answered quietly, "Our omens concern ourselves and our land. They were not meant to foretell the deeds of invaders."

Ka-le had been walking with his eyes to the ground. He had not seen the tall figure standing erect in the center of the yard. Cinque, the speaker's name was, a farmer, ten years older than Ka-le. He had been captured on his way to his new planting field, thrown to the ground, and bound by Arab traders.

Ka-le and Cinque had been chained next to each other on the bench in the slave ship. For the whole time they had sat or crouched side by side. But all that Ka-le knew about Cinque was how he had been taken. It was almost all that any of the captives knew about each other. In the two months spent in the slave ship, there had been little talk of anything except the terrible moment of capture.

The hundred men and women, the boys and young girls had told and retold their tales in the darkness of the ship. Those who had lived to be brought on land again to this slavepen now spent their days recalling their capture:

"They sank my canoe. They came into my house while I was sleeping. They beat me, overpowered me."

"I pawned myself for debt to my neighbor—not to strangers, not to the unspeakable white man. I worked in the fields until my parents paid my debt. They paid ten pieces of cloth and a goat. Ah, but they love me, my parents. On the way home I was beset by Arabs."

On the ship, Cinque had added his own lament to those of his companions: "I was going to my rice fields. If they had not caught my right arm and bound it above my shoulder, if not that—I would not have been made helpless."

But Ka-le had noticed that, in the barracoon, Cinque had ceased to speak of the past. He spent much time in whispered talk with the man who brought them bowls of food.

"The man is of the Mandi tribe; he speaks our language," Cinque had reported one day. Another time, he had said: "We are on an island that has the name of Cuba. The man who holds us captive is a slave dealer. He feeds us well to fatten us. When we have recovered from the voyage, he will sell us."

These facts seemed important to the farmer, but Ka-le and the others received the reports in hopeless silence. Nevertheless, when Cinque spoke, there was no one among the captives who did not listen. Cinque was a man one listened to.

"Do not put the blame of our misfortunes on the omens of our gods," Cinque said now, and touched Ka-le's shoulder gently. "Come over here, to the wall. I will show you something."

The wall of the barracoon was built of wooden boards, not of bricks as walls at home would have been. In one board there was a knothole.

"Rise on tiptoe," whispered Cinque. "Put your eye to the hole. Tell me what you see."

"I see the water, waves of endless water," Ka-le answered after a moment.

"What else?" Cinque persisted.

"Only the sun coming up where sky and water meet." Ka-le was disappointed.

"*Only* the sun!" said Cinque. "Until today I have

not seen the sun rise above the horizon since I saw it over my rice fields. Straight ahead, as you are looking, our homes are waiting, east to the rising sun. We must find some way of returning. We must! Don't look so amazed. Your mother understands this as I do. The thought that you will be free again is all that has kept her alive."

Free? Ka-le turned from the sight of the rising sun, impatiently. He moved his feet so that the chains rattled and grated against the ankle irons. He asked sharply who could break those chains? How would he be brought back home again across the water?

"I do not know," Cinque answered. "But it will be so. It is not right for Mandi to serve as slaves."

2. A Bargain Is Struck

THE morning that had begun so strangely for Ka-le held more surprises. The attendant who came with food was followed by the slave dealer himself. The hard-faced white man ordered the captives to form in line after they had eaten. The Negroes could not understand his words, but the order was repeated by the attendant, he who spoke Mandingo, the Mandi language.

What now? A shiver of dread ran through the slavepen. Any new thing, any change, would probably be for the worse.

Ka-le stumbled to his feet and crept, with what haste his chains would allow, to the side of his mother. She took the arm he offered. But she was too weak to stand. She sank down again to the ground and buried her face.

The slave dealer crossed the yard in long strides. He held a short whip in his hands. But he did not use it. He looked down at the woman, shrugged and turned to order the others forward.

Again his servant repeated the command, in the Mandingo language. Then he added, as if his words were still part of the master's order, "You are to go down to the sea and bathe. He wants you to make a good appearance for what will come after."

Then seeing that Ka-le did not move from his mother's side, the attendant prodded the boy roughly into line. Under the eye of the master, the man made a show of roughness, but he whispered under his breath, "I will stay and tend the woman. Go in peace."

A small gate creaked open. Outside the walls, two white men, with guns, stood on guard. As Ka-le passed through the gate, he noticed that the guards counted on their fingers the number of slaves leaving the yard. He could have told them that the number was fifty-seven. They were the three young girls, Marga, Teme, and Ferni; two older women, not counting his mother; four boys his own age or younger, and forty-seven grown men.

But for all the guards' careful counting, only fifty-six captives returned from the beach. One of the older women simply kept walking in the water until the waves off shore came over her head. She disappeared without a sound before the guards saw what was happening.

The other captives watched with mixed feelings. Tua, an old man, a scholar, cried out and reached with his long arms to try to save her. But others made movements as if to follow the woman's example. For a moment, the example of such an easy death stirred the bathers, like wind sweeping through a field of parched grass.

It was Cinque's voice that broke the spell. "Not that way!" he shouted. "Whom do you cheat if you take your lives by drowning—the kidnapers? You cheat them only of your labor. But you cheat yourselves most of all! The only thing we've got left is our lives. While we live, we have a chance of freedom!"

The white men on guard with their guns came running up at the sound of Cinque's urgent voice. They could not understand what he was saying. They knew nothing of the woman who had drowned herself. But they saw that something was wrong and drove the slaves back into the pen.

In the center of the yard, the Africans saw that a platform had been set up. Near by, the slave dealer stood talking to two strangers in white, tight-fitting clothes and shining boots.

Ka-le's eyes darted from the sight of the strangers to the spot where he had left his mother. But the young girls—Teme, Marga, and Ferni—surrounded her, kneeling on the ground at her feet. The boy could glimpse only her bent head and a fold of her trailing blue garment. With the other captives, Ka-le backed against the wall, as the slave dealer left his companions and strode forward.

The man looked over the huddled group and then pulled one man forward: Komono, a tall silent huntsman with wide tattoo marks on his neck. The slave dealer urged Komono toward the platform. He motioned with the hand that held the whip, for Komono to mount. Then he beckoned the other white men, his customers, to come close to examine and make their offer for this excellent slave.

The younger of the strangers felt of Komono's muscles, examined his scars, his eyes, his teeth. The slave dealer meanwhile kept up a patter of talk in that language none of the Africans could understand.

Komono stepped down from the platform and Pugnaw, the youngest of the boys, took his place. The thin man in leather boots stepped up again. Again the slave dealer began his chatter. . . .

It had come—the selling! What good now was

Cinque's brave talk of freedom, of return to the land of the rising sun? Ka-le kept his back to the wall, and edged slowly away from the group of waiting captives. He crouched low, trying to make himself invisible against the wooden boards. Unnoticed, he crept toward the other side of the yard, toward his mother, until he stood just behind her, with his hands clenched to his sides.

"Sit down and relax!" Señor Montez urged, when he and Ruiz came out to the patio of the hotel at the close of the midday meal.

After his difficult morning's work at the barracoon, the young man would have enjoyed a long quiet rest. To drink something cool and watch the sunlight play over the statues in the garden would be delightful.

"Sit down," his companion repeated lazily. "You have earned a rest. It's not every day you buy fifty blacks with good sound bodies—at bargain prices, too. Your uncle should be grateful."

Ruiz prided himself as a judge of blacks and agreed that he had struck a good bargain. He had caught the fact in time that the older women were not good buys—the one with a bad wound, the other fever-ridden. Since Montez had bid for the three girls, this left only men and boys for him to bargain for. But he had made his uncle's twenty-five thousand pesos go far. He had bought fifty likely laborers. Yet somehow he did not like the tone of Montez' praise.

Ruiz glanced at the older man to see if perhaps he was being made fun of for taking his duties seriously. But Montez looked perfectly friendly as he ordered a long drink and settled back in comfort. He was pleased himself with the morning at the barracoon. He had bought only three slaves, but they were all young healthy girls, who would be useful on his plantation.

"Yes, Pepé," Montez concluded, sipping his drink, "your uncle will say, 'Well done!' "

But Ruiz could not relax. "The work is not complete yet," he answered a little sharply. "You forget that we have not arranged for transport. The blacks must be delivered to Puerto Principe, and we have not found a boat to carry them."

"Transport?" Pedro Montez waved his hand in the direction of the harbor. "That should be simple. Just go down to the water front and see which of the coastwise schooners are in port. We planters give the sea captains our trade all year. It's little enough to ask of them to haul a few slaves around to the other side of the island."

"Simple for you, perhaps," Ruiz persisted. "You have only the three girls to think of. Carrying fifty men and boys fresh from the African voyage is a different matter."

"Nonsense," murmured Montez. "I saw Ramon Ferrer on the Plaza yesterday, with that new young wife of his clinging to his arm. He's got a sugar boat, the *Amistad*. If you must get the matter of transport settled in such a hurry, go down to the harbor and find him. He'll be glad enough to carry our cargo."

Señor Montez stretched his legs out and took a sip of his drink. "Go at once if you must. You are young, Pepé. You'll find that I haven't stirred from this spot when you return."

It was not difficult for Ruiz to locate the long black schooner of Ramon Ferrer, but persuading the captain took all of the young man's powers.

The *Amistad* was a sugar boat, a topsail schooner of about one hundred and twenty tons. She was American-built, though she flew the Spanish flag. Captained by Ramon Ferrer, she had been engaged for six years in a coastwise traffic between Havana and the trading posts in the bays and harbors of Cuba.

Captain Ferrer had always carried sugar, making a certain number of trips each season when the cane was ready for transport. He delivered the fresh-cut canes to the sugar mills in Havana and brought back a cargo of silks, hardware, books— any luxuries the planters ordered from the city. Once in a while a planter or his family would ship as passengers. The captain always made room for them, although the *Amistad* was not a large boat and boasted only two cabins.

Ferrer acted as his own navigator and picked up a fresh crew of two or three sailors for each voyage. It was cheaper to manage in this way, and he had no need for experienced seamen. His trips varied in length from three days to four weeks, depending on the winds, the weather, and the amount of trade. He had never carried slaves, except, of course, his own cook and the cabin boy, Antonio.

The slave trade was profitable, especially since the treaty with Britain made importing Africans unlawful. Since the treaty had gone into effect, many shipowners had made fortunes. The number of captives brought in yearly had almost doubled.

But it had never occurred to Ramon Ferrer to enter the trade. He had no taste for the traffic. Even when hard pressed for money, as he was now, the captain had not thought of transporting slaves on the *Amistad*.

But Señor Ruiz had put the matter very nicely. "I would like to take a few blacks with me down to my uncle's place in Puerto Principe. Would you consider them baggage, for my friend and myself? Señor Pedro Montez, who wants to go along, was sure you would do us this favor. He has made a few purchases in the market himself. The slaves will hardly take more room than a good load of sugar canes."

"A Negro or two," Captain Ferrer replied, "can no doubt be managed."

"Well, to tell the truth, there will be a greater number than that—fifty would be nearer," Ruiz smiled disarmingly.

"Fifty blacks? On the *Amistad*?" Ferrer shook his head.

But Señor Ruiz was not easily discouraged. "Consider them cargo. You travel light down the coast. Not always fully loaded on the return trip either, I would guess."

That was true, Heaven knows! Times were none

too good, especially if one had a wife who liked silk dresses and jewels. And Señor Ruiz was a man worth knowing. Nor would it be bad business to do a favor for Señor Montez.

He would undertake the transport of the slaves, Ferrer agreed, if Señor Ruiz would have food, wooden planks for benches, padlocks, ropes, and everything else in readiness by dark. "The wind being willing," the captain concluded a little abruptly, "the *Amistad* will sail at dawn."

3. The Parting Gift

IRON collars were being fastened with padlocks around the necks of the Africans. Two by two—men to men—boys to boys—they were being yoked for the march to the schooner, through the streets of Havana. Ruiz directed everything, and the slave dealer helped him. His responsibility had really ended when he had received his money in the morning. But for a good customer it paid to be obliging.

The girls of Señor Montez were not yoked. The chains had been taken from their ankles. They were bound only by small arm chains tied to a long rope which Montez already held in readiness for the march.

Making the rest of the slaves secure took longer. The sun had set and dusk was rapidly stealing through the walls of the barracoon. There were still two boys to be padlocked: Pugnaw, age nine, weight sixty pounds; Ka-le, age fifteen, weight ninety pounds.

Ruiz checked off the last names from his list of purchases. The collar was put on Pugnaw's neck and the slave dealer snapped an order to his attendant. The man hurried to bring Ka-le from the corner, where he stood above the women who were being left behind.

"It is time," the man said to Ka-le, in a voice that did not match the pity in his eyes.

Ka-le trembled in his whole body, not so much for himself but for his mother. How would she bear this separation?

But she looked up at him suddenly and her eyes were without fear. "Lean closer," she whispered. "They will not prevent a last farewell."

As he bent down to put his arms around her, Ka-le felt something hard and cold pressed into his ankle. "It's a file, to cut iron." The mother's words were spoken hurriedly. "Who would have thought that I would have something to give you, a parting gift for my son? Do not ask how I got it. Pass it to Cinque when you can. Follow Cinque as you would your father. And if you get home—tell them . . ."

"It is time," the servant broke in nervously when he saw that the file was safely hidden. Then he prodded and pushed the boy across the enclosure, shouting so forbiddingly that he won a nod of approval from the slave dealer. But the scolding tone did not match the words spoken in Mandingo. "Do not grieve," he was saying. "Be comforted. I will care for your mother while she lives."

The big gates to the road were thrown open, and Ruiz, in his white suit and high boots, with a pistol at his belt, led the slaves down the dusty road. Alongside the men walked the slave dealer. He carried his whip and a rifle over his shoulder.

The last pair of men yoked together were Cinque and Goona, a short, heavy man with long hair bound with a leather strap around his brow. Next in line came Pugnaw and Ka-le, then the other young boys. The girls of Señor Montez straggled behind. They had to match their master's slow pace, since Montez held the rope by which they were led.

The procession kept to back streets when the city was reached. But the chained blacks aroused no interest among the passersby. Cubans were used to seeing slaves marched to the water front for shipment, in the dusk of early evening. The mile-and-a-half walk to the harbor where the *Amistad* was docked passed without incident. The few words Ka-le spoke in Cinque's ear went unnoticed.

Ruiz and the slave dealer stood at the gangplank, motioning the Negroes forward with clear-cut gestures. It was a nuisance that none of them understood the Spanish language, but the slave dealer managed to get them started up the gangplank.

As soon as Montez arrived, Ruiz ran ahead to get the first slaves down between decks. He showed Captain Ferrer and one of the crew how to fasten the Negroes to the benches which had been set up. Long ropes, run through the iron collars and padlocked to the benches, made them quite secure. Then the young man hurried back up to the deck to lean against the rail and watch the rest of his purchases come on board.

At the waterside, a small incident caused some delay. The boys, who followed the grown men, had crowded a little too closely. One of the last men stumbled. Because of the rope that yoked him to his companion, the other man staggered, too, and almost fell.

Cinque was the name of the slave who had stumbled and was now being helped up by the boys. Ruiz remembered that the sleek brown-skinned farmer had stalked up to the slave block as though his ankle chain weighed no more than a spider web. But he looked clumsy enough now, Heaven knows!

The space set aside for the Negroes ran the width of the ship in back of the cook's galley. It was about four and a half feet high and was lined with the hastily constructed benches. There was room for eight slaves to a bench. But it proved difficult to crowd all fifty into the space. The last two men and also the girl slaves of Pedro Montez were left over.

Ruiz padlocked the two men to the deck below the forecastle, where the captain agreed they would give no trouble. The three girls, who wore only arm chains, were free to run the deck. But they huddled, instead, at the foot of the one called Cinque, as though riveted to his ankle chain.

Montez was disgusted. He had told them in every language he could think of that there was nothing to be afraid of. Ruiz shrugged off his friend's impatience. Everything would be all right, he felt, as soon as the schooner was out of the harbor and on the open sea.

But the *Amistad* did not put to sea that night. At the last minute Captain Ferrer refused to sail without papers. He demanded passports for transporting the Negroes. He refused to raise anchor until proper passports were provided for carrying slaves from one end of the island to the other. For the honor of his ship, the captain insisted on having everything in order.

There was nothing wrong, he said, in transporting the slaves of the señores. Therefore one must not let carelessness give the appearance of wrong. After all, there were three British cruisers in the harbor for the purpose of searching suspected slave ships. There was also the Britisher, Dr. Madden, sitting in his courtroom in Havana, with authority to seize any vessel that carried captive Bozals.

"The devil take Dr. Madden!" cried Ruiz.

"If only the devil would," Ramon Ferrer answered agreeably. He added that the *Amistad* was well known as a sugar boat and not likely to be stopped for search. Nevertheless he would not raise anchor until the papers were in his hands.

"Your crew will not enjoy watching the night through with a bunch of Africans aboard in the harbor," Montez remarked.

Ferrer looked aft toward the two seamen. They had been signed on only the day before. They were fair-skinned, yellow-haired—Danes perhaps or Yankees. Foreigners in any case. The captain patted the gun at his belt. "I am not accustomed to trouble with crews, señor."

"Quite so!" Ruiz gave in with sudden grace, motioned Montez to lead the way down the gangplank, and went ashore.

It was all very well, Ruiz grumbled, for Ramon Ferrer to want things in order. The captain of the *Amistad* didn't have to sit around waiting for a government clerk to prepare passports. Nor did he have to write down all sorts of useless information and remember to put Ladinos in every spot instead of Bozals, as Nicholas Trist had recommended.

It was four o'clock in the afternoon before Ruiz and Montez had the papers in hand and were ready to make their way back to the *Amistad*. Furthermore they were greeted with the news that one of the Negroes had died, and the body thrown overboard was inviting the unpleasant company of sharks.

"Died from no discoverable cause," Captain Ferrer made a careful report. "My cook says the man was of the Masai tribe. No good as slaves. In slavery or in prison, they simply die. Most of the rest, he says, are Mandi. A very good tribe."

"Is the cook a Mandi?" Ruiz asked.

"Selestino, you mean?" The captain looked up in surprise. "My cook? I have never asked. I have had him for many years, and Antonio, my cabin boy, was born into slavery in my mother's household."

Señor Ruiz was not interested in the history of Captain Ferrer's servants. He merely wanted to know if the cook could speak the language of his own slaves. If so, he wanted the man to tell them to stop their wailing.

"Ask them if they have a singing man," Ruiz said, when the cook was called. "Tell them to stop that wailing and sing."

"They wail for the dead, señor," Selestino answered indifferently. "For two days they must mourn, since it was an old man that died. If it had been a woman, the mourning would last three days, because man was made before woman."

"You heard the señor," the captain said shortly. "Tell the blacks to keep silent or sing. Of course," sighed Ferrer, "they have just arrived from a barbaric land. The one that died," he let his gaze rest briefly on the water with its attendant shark, "the dead one had a heathen charm about his neck, the size of a hen's egg. He had grasped the barbaric thing with both hands, before he died." The captain frowned at the distasteful memory. "How fortunate these heathens are," he remarked, "to have come to a civilized land, where decent ways will be taught them!"

As the journey progressed, Captain Ferrer was further convinced of the good fortune of the slaves. Though they did not work at all, and nothing was expected of them except to sit quietly until it was time for them to be brought on deck for their exercise, they were fed the most generous amounts of rice and water twice a day.

"You take very good care of them, señor," Ferrer said to Ruiz, as the young man stood over the silent pair on the forward deck to see that they ate their food.

But for all the care given them, on the evening of the fourth day, another captive died. Just when the worst of the journey was done and the ship had rounded the tip of the island and was headed straight west for Puerto Principe!

This time it was the long-haired man on the deck who died. He had called himself Goona, and Ruiz had paid four hundred pesos for him. A mountain Negro, according to the slave dealer at the barracoon, from the high mountains, inland from Lomboko. He had been recommended especially for his great strength. Now he was dead, and the money paid for him might as well have been thrown in the ocean.

The great weight of the body made it hard to

handle. When Ruiz unlocked the padlock that bound him to his companion, the body fell forward and lay half across Cinque, the living slave. Cinque leaped out of the way as far as his chain would let him, while the girls shrank back, whimpering.

Ruiz nodded toward the water. "Cast the body overboard," he directed.

Cinque looked at the white man when he spoke, but he did not move.

"When they don't want to do something they pretend not to understand!" Ruiz sputtered. Then he repeated the demand somewhat louder, as one does to a person who is hard of hearing.

The Negro only stared. He had pulled himself up to his full height and had to look down to meet the eyes of the white man.

"Tell him he is to throw that body overboard," the captain said to his cook, who had appeared with Antonio from the galley.

Ruiz watched the exchange of words between the two, impatiently. "He understood all right. He's just stubborn. Those fine-looking blacks are always hard to handle. I paid a crazy high price for him, too."

"He says he will not." The cook spoke softly, ne-

glecting to add that Cinque had explained that it
was forbidden to touch the dead.

The body from which life has fled must be
placed on a mat made of palm leaves. The head
must be turned to the falling sun and a bowl of rice
placed beside it. The spirit of the dead must not
go hungry. But these rites are to be undertaken only
by an old woman of the tribe or by someone close
of kin. To all others, it is forbidden to touch a
corpse. Cinque had reminded Selestino of the well-
known taboo, but the cook well knew that the white
men would not be interested.

"He will not! Santa Maria!" Captain Ferrer was
accustomed to being obeyed.

"The dead man is not of my family," Cinque
spoke in a strong clear voice. "He has three wives
and seven children and a father and three sisters
back in the mountains where he was captured. Any
one of them could have given Goona burial rites.
But I am no kin."

"What does he say?" Ruiz interrupted. One had
to be careful when slaves spoke together in a
strange tongue.

"Just that he will not obey you, señor. Shall I get
the whip?" Selestino was not sorry to see this proud
newcomer taught a lesson.

"Antonio will fetch it," Captain Ferrer spoke regretfully. A scene like this was not seemly on the *Amistad*. It was always distressing when punishment had to be applied. He pitied Señor Ruiz sincerely.

Ruiz was less disturbed. Flogging was part of everyday business. It was simply his duty to make plain that he was master of this new-bought slave.

When the whip was brought and the flogging was finished, Cinque stood on the deck with hanging arms and head. Such a deep watchful look of sadness passed over his face, that the captain felt at his belt to make sure of his gun. He did not know what the next moment might bring forth.

But the slave only snapped his fingers. Then, without a waste motion, as you would hoist a bundle of canes or that pile of sugar knives stacked on the deck, he took Goona's body in his arms. He lifted it above the rail and let it slide from his arms down to the upreaching sea.

The white, foamy waves beat against the sides of the ship. The three girls broke into a low wail, and that was the only sound to be heard. But on his way back to the galley, Selestino muttered, "The slave snapped his fingers—a Mandi only snaps his fingers in despair."

4. "Throw Them Bread"

ANTONIO, the cabin boy, pushed open the trap door between the cook's galley and the dark, dank quarters of Señor Ruiz' slaves. The shaft of light from behind shone on the faces of the Africans and told the boy at once that these stupid creatures knew nothing of the happening on deck.

They were sitting quite still on the benches, more like things of stone than like people. They did not even look up when he appeared with a bucket of water and rice bowls. Only the young one, back in the corner, was chattering to the tall boy they called Ka-le. And Ka-le sat silent, with his fists clenched against his thighs.

So much had been going on, and these Bozals knew nothing! Antonio had the greatest contempt for the Africans. They could not understand the simplest order given by a white man. They had nothing to wear but iron chains and loincloths.

Antonio wore the livery of Captain Ramon Ferrer
—purple breeches and a yellow shirt and long
white stockings. His livery was not just a covering
for his body. It clothed his mind and feelings as
well. He had been born into slavery in the Ferrer
household and had been raised to become the captain's body servant. He belonged to Captain Ferrer
with his whole heart.

Antonio used his eyes only to see the things his
master wanted seen. His memory served only to
store up tales to tell that would bring praise and
attention from the master. His feelings were either
pride or shame—pride if he had satisfied, shame if
he had the misfortune to displease the captain.

This last seldom happened. Antonio was very
shrewd about putting himself in the sunlight of his
master's approval. If there were no ways of getting
his master's attention, he manufactured them. But
since the beginning of this voyage he had felt himself neglected in favor of Selestino. It was Selestino
whom the captain called on because Selestino knew
the language of the Bozals.

As if Antonio could not speak to them too—a
little anyhow! Even before—and much more in
the last few days—he had learned Mandi words
from the cook. Soon he would let Captain Ferrer

hear him speak the Bozal's language. Then the master would let Antonio give the orders.

Perhaps the moment had come, Antonio thought, as he scampered back and forth bringing the bowls of food. He could startle these ignorant Bozals with his tale of the events on the deck and then report to Captain Ferrer anything wrong they said or did. The captain would smile and say, "Well done!" —or even give him a sweetmeat from the box on his desk!

Antonio stopped in front of Ka-le and the skinny young one, yoked to him, who was still chattering like a monkey. "What a pity," Antonio said softly, "you were not above to see the beating! I brought the whip . . ."

Pugnaw's chatter ceased. Antonio waited for questions. None came, so he went on with his story. "That Cinque got a good beating because he would not throw the body of the dead one overboard."

"Who has died?" Ka-le's fingernails bit into his tight-closed hands. Was it Marga? Teme? . . . the names of the girls who had been so kind to his mother flashed into his mind.

But it was not the young girls who had died. Antonio continued in a blustering voice, "Goona, the long-haired, died. The sharks have him now. It did no good for Cinque to refuse the master's bidding. He just got a beating, and then he had to cast the body overboard after all. Then Señor Ruiz fastened Cinque's chains to the deck again. But before that, the Bozal snapped his fingers. When a Mandi snaps his fingers, Selestino says, it means trouble."

Antonio looked around hopefully. That would be something to tell Captain Ferrer if it was true. But the captives disappointed him. No one answered. No one made a sound, not even a wail for the dead. They just sat still with the rice bowls in their hands.

"Oh, well," Antonio said to himself, "just three more days and we'll be rid of the lot of them." He closed the trap door and pranced up on deck for a little fresh air in his nostrils before it was time to serve supper to the captain and the señores.

The silence continued for many minutes after the cabin boy had closed the trap door. No one spoke Goona's name in the darkness, because to speak the name of the dead disturbs the spirit that has left the body. But presently Tua recalled in low, despairing tones all they knew of the dead man.

"Slavers set fire to his village, high in the mountains. When the people ran out of the burning houses, they were taken prisoner. Of all from that village, only the long-haired one weathered the ocean voyage. And now his body lies in the water. He was a stranger to the water . . ."

A low wailing began. Suddenly Fulway, the maker of charms, lifted his wooden bowl, still full of rice, and flung it to the floor.

"Do not mourn the dead," Fulway cried. "Mourn for us, the living. Cinque is beaten with a whip, like an ox in his field. What has happened to Cinque will happen to us all!" He jerked a charm from around his neck and hurled it after the bowl of rice.

"Poor Cinque and his talk of freedom . . ." That was Grabeau speaking. Ka-le recognized the voice, though he could not see the man's heavy-set, strong-muscled figure in the darkness. But he could hear him beating against the iron collar around his throat. Grabeau had a hatred of the irons beyond all the others. A hatred lay between him and the cold metal, as if the thing he knew best had betrayed him. Grabeau was a blacksmith.

Perhaps, thought Ka-le, I should have given the file to Grabeau. But his mother had said to give it to Cinque, and he had done this, on the water front, just before they entered the ship. Then after all Cinque had been left on the deck, separated from his companions.

Ka-le had said nothing of the file to the others. Away from Cinque, courage and hope had faded, and the gift of his mother seemed a worthless thing. But now, the boy thought, it should be mentioned.

"Grabeau," he asked, "do you know the tool called a file?"

"Of course," the man answered. "Should not an ironworker know his tools? A file is for cutting."

"Cinque has a file," Ka-le said softly.

"Cinque?"

At the tone of the blacksmith's voice, Ka-le's blood tingled. "It is hidden in his ankle iron," he said. "My mother gave it to me, a parting gift. I passed it to Cinque at the water's edge. That time he—and the long-haired one—pretended to stumble . . . in that moment Cinque hid the file!"

"Cinque has a file!" Grabeau's chain rattled in the dark, and his voice was like a drumbeat. Suddenly he bent over his untouched bowl of rice. "Eat," he whispered fiercely, "eat and grow strong. Cinque has a file for cutting through iron. And you heard what that monkey of a boy in white men's garments said—Cinque snapped his fingers!"

The sun had set abruptly, without any grand display of fireworks. The captain turned over the wheel to one of the crew and went aft to take the log. Seven knots . . . the schooner was not making bad progress. But Ramon Ferrer was impatient to see the end of this voyage. He returned to the helm and ordered the crew to let out more sail.

After a supper eaten without conversation, the two passengers retired to their quarters. The captain went presently to his own cabin to write up his logbook: "The thirtieth of June, 1839. Fourth day out. Ninety leagues from port. Wind E. by S.E. seven knots. Slave of Señor Ruiz died. Corpse overboard. No special happenings."

This being done, Ferrer opened the velvet case that held the portrait of his wife. It was a handsome case with a clasp of silver, unsuited to the rough surroundings of a cabin on a coastwise sugar schooner. The captain prized it the more because it was a present from his young wife. She had picked out the case on their wedding afternoon and placed the portrait within, with her own hands.

She was a lover of beautiful things—and costly ones! The sea captain sighed. He had not been able, in the months since their wedding, to give her the many trinkets she had admired. There was, in particular, a pair of earrings fashioned of little seed pearls.

"Are they not beautiful, Ramon?" his wife had said in the shop in a little side street off the Plaza. "And a bargain besides!"

"Madame Ferrer is a judge of fine jewels," the shopkeeper had urged.

But Ramon Ferrer had been forced to admit that his profits from the last voyage were too small to allow him to buy the earrings. It had been a great sorrow, especially when he saw the disappointment in his wife's eyes. Now, with the money paid for transporting the slaves of Señor Ruiz, the jewels could be purchased. When her disappointment turned to joy, all the trouble with these blacks would seem worth while!

The captain took off his boots and lay down. He needed to get some sleep before the dawn watch, when he would relieve his crew.

But it was hot and stuffy in the cabin. Ferrer could not sleep, and about midnight he clapped for his cabin boy, who slept outside his door. He had Antonio carry his pallet to the deck, amidship.

Even here on deck the night was hot. The sky was overcast with a mist the color of sulphur on the horizon. The world beyond the deck of the *Amistad* appeared vast and silent. Ramon Ferrer thought again of his wife and the earrings he would buy for her.

Then he slept heavily until he was awakened by Antonio tugging at his sleeve. This must have been between three and four in the morning, for the moon was scurrying out of its clouds when Captain Ferrer opened his eyes. And the time for the moon to rise, on this night of the thirtieth of June, 1839, was a little after three.

At first the seaman thought he must be dreaming. A white form like a huge bird was visible overhead. Then the figure seemed to take the shape of a man. Ferrer opened his eyes wider and saw that there was indeed a man, high on the rigging.

Antonio's voice was close to his ear, "The Bozals have risen! Cinque and Tua and Komono, the tattooed one."

"The slaves?" The captain couldn't believe his ears. "They are chained!"

"Those padlocks are nothing." Antonio talked fast. At last he had his master's full attention. "The chain was cut with a file in the hands of the one on deck, called Cinque. Don't you remember Selestino said there would be trouble when the Mandi snapped his fingers? That's what Selestino said."

Ferrer was on his feet now. "Where is Selestino?"

Antonio pointed. The shadow on the rigging was outlined sharply in the moonlight. White trousers flapped like misplaced jib sails. The cook's tall cap had fallen forward. His arms swung in outlandish position. Below, on the deck, squatted the long-armed Tua.

"He is called 'the ugly one,' " Antonio whispered. Tua held a sugar knife high above his shoulder. The moonlight turned the knife blade to blue fire.

"After Cinque freed himself, he sent the girls below with the file and those sugar knives Señor Ruiz left on deck," Antonio continued monotonously.

Captain Ferrer wrenched himself loose from Antonio and bellowed out the names of the sailors.

But Antonio whispered in his stubborn monotone, "Cinque talked to the sailors. He tried to order them to sail the ship to his homeland, but they could not understand him. They were stupid. Cinque stood above the sailors, and they lashed the tiller rope to the wheel and let down the small boat and fled in the water. It was the noise of their boat being lowered that woke Selestino. But I was already awake! I stayed to see what was happening, so I could tell you, my master."

The captain gave a shout that echoed below,

rousing murmurs like the cries of water fowls or like the grating of a boat on rocky sand. There was the sound of running feet and Cinque appeared in the hatch.

His iron collar was still hanging from his shoulder. The broken chain that had bound him to the deck clanged crazily. In his hand he carried a sugar knife. He spoke a word, and two more figures stood beside him.

"He says the men are breaking their chains," Antonio whispered. "What should I do?"

Captain Ferrer had his hand on his gun, ready for use. But he paused and said a curious thing.

"Throw them bread, Antonio," he ordered, and stood and waited while the boy scurried down the hatch.

The captain waited. And Cinque and Komono and Fulway, his companions, waited like the towers of some ancient fort or like trees in a forest. Above their heads the frightened cook moved a handsbreath. Tua raised the knife higher, circling his long arm from the shoulder. But before he could throw the weapon, Selestino swerved backward, turned, all arms and legs, and settled with a wild shrill cry in the foaming water.

The captain pulled his gun and aimed it point-

blank at the tallest of the men in the hatchway. Komono crumpled and fell to the deck without a sound.

Tua whirled, leaped across the deck, and snatched the weapon before Ferrer could fire again. Tua aimed it at its owner, but Cinque spoke in a tone of command.

"He is for me," Cinque said.

Carefully he measured the distance between himself and the Spaniard, and lifted his body on his toes, like a dancer. Then he folded his right hand a little more firmly around the sugar knife he was carrying and struck the captain. He was standing now above Ferrer, so that the knife entered the body between the shoulder blades. The captain fell forward without speaking another word.

Antonio reported the whole thing afterward. "'Throw them bread,' my master said, but they would not touch it. Then, just as I come back on deck, Selestino falls and my master shoots and Cinque raises his knife, the kind for cutting sugar cane. In one moment my master is no longer in the land of the living. He does not speak after he tells me 'throw them bread.'"

The girls had been sent below decks, but now they came pattering up the gangway to Cinque.

They knelt before him, and their hands fluttered toward him.

"Do not touch me," he said. He looked down at his empty hands. The knife he had thrown was still in the corpse, thrust deep between the shoulders. There was a little blood on the deck, but none at all on Cinque's hands. He held them to the moonlight and examined them.

"I have never killed a man before," he said in a troubled tone.

"It was I who snatched his weapon! I helped," Tua said sharply. "It was not your deed alone."

When Tua spoke, his lips shrank back from two long teeth. He had a deep scar in the center of his forehead between his eyes, and his arms were so long they hung below his knees. It was no wonder that he was nicknamed "the ugly one."

Yet of all those on board Tua was the gentlest. He was a scholar who spoke three languages: Mandingo, Bantu, and Arabic. He understood the thing that troubled the young farmer who was the leader in this uprising. "I helped to kill," he insisted.

"No!" Cinque spoke with authority. "The white men have a custom that I found out in the barracoon, in that town of theirs, Havana. When there is a killing of a white man, his family do not exact money in payment as we do. They do not say, 'This life was worth so many leopard skins, so much cattle.' They kill the killer."

"What good does that do?" Fulway asked. "It is a crazy custom."

"That may be," Cinque shrugged his shoulders. "They kill by hanging. I knew this when I persuaded you to rise and take possession of this vessel. If we do not succeed, if we are captured, it must be well known by all that I am the killer. Then I alone will be hanged. I have thought it out carefully. This thought does not pain me. Throw that weapon far away. We have no need of it."

"So be it." Fulway had not moved from his place in the hatchway. He stepped on the deck now, shrugging his shoulders impatiently. "The ship is ours now. What does it matter how the thing was done? *They* did not ask how many lives they took— those men who bought and sold us."

The pistol hung loosely in Tua's hands. He tightened his fingers around it and moved to the rail to throw.

Antonio watched, fascinated, to see the captain's gun in a black man's hands, to be pitched overboard in the water. Of course, he thought, Señor Montez and Señor Ruiz would have others.

The cabin boy must have spoken the names aloud, because Tua stopped, his arm in midair. "The other white men!" Tua said. "We still have to deal with them!"

"The masters. I had forgotten." Cinque shook himself, and his loose chain rattled. "Since the last link of my chain was broken, I have thought only of the end of this voyage."

"Masters," Fulway whispered bitterly. "Say rather devils in tight breeches and shining boots." He bent down and chose a sugar knife from the pile stacked at his feet.

"I think they will give you all a good beating," Antonio murmured.

His sympathies were not clearly with one side or the other. He was simply stating the way things were—or had been in the world of Captain Ramon Ferrer. He looked down at the captain's corpse in its whiteness; and he remembered, with a tingling of his skin, the body of Selestino falling through the night from the rigging. These two had made up Antonio's world, and they were gone. Between the Bozals and the Spaniards in the cabin, he took neither one side nor the other.

"Where do they sleep?" asked Fulway, testing the blade of the knife on his fingers.

"Down and beyond," Cinque gestured vaguely. "Even so," he said, "if we explain to them, we may need to have no more killing. Surely they could understand that we want to go back to our country . . . if we could speak with them."

"*If* we could speak!" To the scholarly Tua, that was perhaps the hardest thing to bear: to find oneself without a means of being understood.

"I will speak to the whites!" Antonio stammered. Events had convinced him that it would pay to get on the good side of these towering Bozals, at least until the señores could be wakened. Then, no doubt, the world would be turned right side up again.

5. Cinque at the Helm

THE passageway to the Spaniards' cabin led past the cook's galley, whose door was swinging open. Selestino's empty hammock hung in the far corner. A night candle sputtered in a glass and threw lumpy shadows across the threshold. In his haste to be gone, the cook had overturned a water bucket. The water swished back and forth with every jerky motion of the ship, as it plowed, unguided, through the sea.

Antonio stopped at the galley door and looked back at the three armed men behind him. When they had started down the ladder through the hatch, Fulway had motioned the cabin boy ahead.

Fulway was not trusting, like Tua, nor confident, like Cinque. He was a townsman, older than the other two. His brown face was too thin, the narrow cheekbones had the flesh drawn tightly. There was a scar across one cheek, where the Arabs had

slashed when they captured him and sold him into
slavery. He was a sculptor as well as a maker of
charms and he held the clumsy sugar knife as
though it were a sculptor's tool.

At the end of the passageway was the closed door
of the white men's cabin. Threads of light showed
above and around the door. Confused sounds
floated out.

"The men are awake. They have heard something!" Cinque took a place close to the door and
waited.

At Fulway's prodding, Antonio called softly,
"Señor!"

"What the devil is it?" Montez answered, his
voice thick and fuzzy with sleep. "I thought I heard
a pistol shot."

"A little mutiny, señor," Antonio said, with Tua's
hand on his shoulder.

"Mother of Heaven!" Montez did not sound
really disturbed.

"Mutiny!" The voice of Señor Ruiz was sharper.
"I never did like the looks of those yellow-haired
foreign sailors. Ferrer was so sure he could manage
them! Call the captain, boy. Tell him to come
down here."

"Why do you shout so, Pepé?" The older man

could be heard shifting in his bunk. "Mutiny on shipboard is the captain's affair, not ours."

"I've got twenty-five thousand pesos worth of slaves on this schooner," Señor Ruiz answered Montez. Then he raised his voice to Antonio, "Call the captain, I tell you!"

"He cannot come. He is dead, señor." Antonio spoke in a cajoling voice. The three Africans waited patiently behind him.

"The sailors then!" Ruiz shouted. "Send somebody!"

"They are gone, and the cook too." Antonio began to enjoy the effect his words were making. "It is not the crew that has made the mutiny, señores."

Pedro Montez let out a squeal of alarm. "It's the slaves, you fool! Your precious blacks! Lock the door, push that chair against it, Pepé! We are going to be killed! That boy is not alone!"

"You are right, señor," Antonio came closer to the door and spoke through the keyhole. "Cinque is here, and Tua, and the one they call Fulway. They want to sail the *Amistad* back to their own country. They want you to show them how to sail a ship. They bid me say they are here peacefully to have palaver with you."

"Palaver the devil!" Ruiz snorted.

"They say they will show you the way, by the sun," Antonio continued.

There was tumult in the cabin. Montez' voice rose shrilly. "To Africa! I'll not do it, though they kill me and cut me in pieces and feed me to the sharks."

Antonio cajoled, "They say it is right that they should go to their homes. They want the ship turned to the sun." The boy felt Tua's fingers pressing into his arm. He fell silent to hear what Ruiz was saying. Suddenly he flattened himself against the wall. "They are going to shoot!"

The door opened, and the crack of light became a blinding flame in the darkness. Cinque darted full at the opening. With his knife he struck Montez a glancing blow on the arm. With his free hand he sent Ruiz' pistol spinning across the threshold. Montez' gun dropped from his grasp. Cinque kicked it out into the passage. He leaped back and the door slammed shut again.

It was over very quickly. In the darkness of the passage Tua clutched his stomach and groaned. The white man's bullet had not missed. Three guns lay on the floor, that of Montez still smoking and sending off the sour smell of burned powder.

"Throw those weapons over the water," Cinque

commanded, as Fulway bent to gather them in his hands. "We will barricade this door."

Cinque worked silently, using whatever movables he could lay his hands on in the cluttered passageway. From within the cabin flowed a stream of violent sounds.

"That is the voice of the old man," Fulway said. "Now it is the one called Pepé. They bellow like elephants in the jungle before daybreak. What will we do with them? You should have killed them, Cinque, when you had the chance. We could break this door down now and have it over with!"

But Cinque shook his head. "When we come home they can have their ship back again. We will not need it once we have set foot on earth that is our earth."

The young farmer gravely lifted Tua and motioned Antonio and Fulway to follow, leaving behind the confused shouts of the white men.

By the light of the candle burning in the cook's galley, Grabeau worked furiously, filing Ka-le's leg chains. Ka-le and Pugnaw were still yoked together, and Grabeau's own neck was still encircled with an iron collar. But once the ropes that bound the captives to the benches had been cut, they could move

about freely. Even in this narrow space they could breathe the air of freedom, and Grabeau worked with a blacksmith's skill to get rid of the chains.

Pugnaw's ankles were already free. Now the chain on Ka-le's legs gave way with a clang. Grabeau pushed the boys toward the door. "Go up," he said. "The yoke will come off later. Go up and bring us news."

Through the swishing water on the floor of the cook's galley, up the steep ladder, and through the open hatch the two boys clattered. Their legs were free, they scarcely felt the yoke that bound them together.

On deck, the night had given way to the gray and purple dawnlight. The body of the captain lay near the hatchway. Little drops of blood had dried on his white coat, stiffening the edges of cloth where the knife thrust had gone in. One arm had fallen against the cheek of Komono's corpse.

Komono was dead! And, beyond, Ka-le could see Cinque tending Tua, a wounded Tua, who did not speak. Near by stood the girls and that boy who had brought food. Fulway stood by the rail, holding a clumsy knife and the white men's weapons.

Cinque turned his face toward Fulway. "Tua will live," he said. "Throw those weapons far over the water. There must not be any more killing."

Ka-le and Pugnaw moved forward. Marga caught sight of them and darted to Ka-le's side. No word was spoken. They could have been ghosts in the gray light.

Out of the hatchway strode another captive, free of chains. And another! Grabeau's work was going swiftly now.

There was a rush of clanking chains up the hatchway. Grabeau himself came out into the air, armed with his precious file. With daybreak, the open deck was better for his work. He filed like one possessed, freeing his fellow captives.

The corpse of Komono, the hunter, and that of the captain were stiffening a few yards away. As the men came up from below and saw that Komono was dead, some set up a quiet wailing. But none offered to touch the bodies or prepare Komono for burial. No old woman was present, no close kin.

Suddenly Ka-le saw Fulway come from the rail. "Komono's mountains were my mountains," the man said. "His lands were watered by the river Say-wa-ye, where I was born. In these things he was my kinfolk. I will prepare Komono for burial. But what about this white man? Who will prepare his rice bowl? Those others—back there in the cabin—they are not wailing his death, I can tell you. They have taken no thought of burial rites."

Cinque left Tua's side. "They are prisoners," he said shortly. "As for this one, I killed him. I will bury him."

Tua stirred and opened his eyes. "I take some credit for that killing," he said.

"You go to sleep, Tua. Do not concern yourself with my responsibilities." Cinque pushed his way into the circle around the corpses and knelt to his task.

Grabeau scarcely looked up. He kept on filing. He was not turned from his battle with the cold iron by the living or by the dead. He beckoned Ka-le and Pugnaw to come closer and began freeing the boys of their yoke. "We shall need you," he said. "Nimble feet will be needed to climb up the ropes to those tall posts called the masts."

Because Grabeau was a blacksmith, he had also been a traveler. A worker in iron must go far seeking metal. In the forty years of his lifetime he had crossed deserts and rivers, and had seen the boats of the white men on wide waters. He understood the matter of sails and masts and rigging. Grabeau had seen the sailship *Tecora* in the Lomboko harbor with a red flag hung out that meant "good trading." He had paddled out in a small boat to have a look at it, and that is how he had been captured.

The schooner, of which they had taken possession, would have to have sailors. Daylight was breaking. Soon the sun would be rising. Then the ship must be turned in the direction of the rising sun. Grabeau worked to free those who would be most helpful.

Ka-le stood patiently under the grating file, and watched Cinque and Fulway at their preparations. He saw Teme go down the ladder with Antonio and bring back bowls of rice and two spoons. He saw the bodies of the dead laid out side by side and covered with sailcloth.

There was good light to see by now. Below the edge of the water one became aware of the presence of the sun.

Cinque turned away from his completed task and came to watch Grabeau. The blacksmith did not pause in his filing. He scowled and said, "Fulway has told me that those in the cabin, sons of lizards, have refused to guide the ship through the water."

Cinque nodded. "It is so. We shall have to guide it ourselves." He spoke serenely. What had to be done would be done.

"The white man's ship is not a canoe that can be sent through the water at the touch of a paddle," Grabeau said. "It is a stubborn and willful beast that requires hard riding. I have seen boats before."

"I know," Cinque answered. "Give over the filing to some of the others. You alone know about boats, except what I have learned watching the yellow-haired sailors when I was chained to the deck. We have to turn the front end of the boat to the sun, Grabeau. We must face the rising sun."

There were a dozen outstretched hands for the file. Grabeau gave it into the care of a young man called Bau, and showed him how to hold the tool so it would bite through the iron. Then he strode off with Cinque to the back of the vessel, where the tiller rope was lashed to the helm.

Some followed the two men to the bow of the ship. But others remained, waiting their turn to be freed of chains or staring down at the bodies of the dead. Antonio was one of these last. He would have liked some share in the burial rites of his master. But he did not know what to do about it.

The ceremonies of the Africans held no meaning for him. And the customs of the Spanish world, into which he had been born a slave, were almost as meaningless. Yet when he saw the body of Ramon Ferrer, with the life gone out, Antonio had a desire to perform some rite of farewell.

He started uncertainly to make the sign of the Cross, but there was no one to say whether this was right or appropriate. So he let his hand fall to his side again. The sailcloth covering had blown off the captain's face. The staring eyes were closed now. Ramon Ferrer's face looked gray, like stone.

There was one thing Antonio could do that had never failed to please his master. The boy's eyes searched out a clear spot on the deck. His right arm swept upward, then curved down in a wide half-circle. His head and shoulders swayed forward, and he turned a perfect cart wheel. Then another and another. The captain was always very fond of cart wheels!

The Africans watched. Their gaze followed Antonio's movements with curiosity. The wailing was hushed, and in the stillness Ferni laughed. Ferni, the little frog, the gay one!

A wave of uneasiness swept over the boatload of freed men. Someone had laughed! In all the weeks since they had been torn from their homes, not a laugh had been heard among them. They stood rigid at the sound of the laughter. But no cloud came to darken the morning sky. The surf that beat against the sides of the white man's ship did not rise to engulf them. Nothing happened to forbid a child's laughter.

"Point the boat homeward, toward the sun!" A child has laughed. It is good to be free!

6. East, by the Sun

RUIZ had heard the Negroes leave the passage outside the cabin, but he had continued to pile boxes and chairs against the door for safety. Montez had ceased to move about. He sat on the edge of his bunk and hugged his bleeding arm against his side.

"I shall most likely die of loss of blood before daylight. But you do not care! You have not even offered to put a bandage on my wound."

Ruiz did not answer, and Montez went on complaining. "Shoot your way out! That was a fine idea, wasn't it? What are you doing with all that furniture? It's too late for barricades. Mother of Heaven! Let the savages come in and make an end to us. I shall bleed to death in any case."

"A scratch, that's all you've got! For heaven's sake stop whining," Ruiz muttered.

"You think I'm a coward? You and your twenty-five thousand pesos worth of blacks!" Montez began shouting oaths at Ferrer and his crew that could not be trusted.

"If I had wanted to run the risk of traveling with a lot of unguarded savages, I could have chartered a boat and taken it down the island myself. I used to be master of a vessel. I'm as good a navigator as Ramon Ferrer was any day."

Ruiz snorted impatiently. "Why didn't you take charge, then, when that cabin boy asked you to?"

"And sail to Africa? Mother of Heaven!" Montez cried.

"How would those blacks know where the boat was heading?"

"They know the direction. Do you think I want to get myself killed when they discover that I'm sailing away from the morning sun? If I were a young man, I'd go out barehanded and whip those slaves back into their quarters."

"They'll be flogged quite thoroughly when we get to land." Ruiz spoke dreamily. The thought of taking the whip to Cinque was a soothing pleasure.

"Land? What land? Didn't you understand their purpose?"

"I heard what the cabin boy said. It was just a trick to get us outside. We're headed west, away from Africa, aren't we?"

"South by west," Montez answered. "I reckon us to be about three days away from Puerto Principe. They'd have to put the ship about, against the current. That's no easy thing."

"They can't do it, of course." Ruiz was confident. "How can savages handle a boat? Did they learn navigation in the jungle? We'll drift along until some vessel passes. Then we'll signal for help and have the blacks taken to the nearest port for flogging."

"More likely to Havana to be hanged for Ferrer's murder," Montez chuckled. "If we are rescued, you'll see your valuable blacks hanging from the gallows."

"In that case the government would pay me back, don't you think? Slaves rising during transport can't be tolerated. Nobody could go safely from one plantation to another."

A difficulty occurred to the older man. "And how will you hail a vessel? Who will see you, down in this cabin? Besides, we're not drifting. I can feel."

Ruiz went to the tiny porthole and climbed on a stool and stuck his head out. "Those sailors must have lashed the tiller rope when they deserted.

We're keeping our course. The blacks can't do anything about it."

"If they try to put about with the wind, they'll snap a mast. If they try to jibe, we'll likely go over on our side. We are carrying eighty yards of sail. That's no plaything in ignorant hands."

Montez would have explained the problems of sailing a schooner at further length, but just then he noticed several drops of fresh blood on his arm. The dangers of the sea were nothing to him compared to the sight of his own blood dripping away. He let himself down tenderly in his bunk.

The boat had begun to list to leeward. It was all he could do to keep from rolling against the wall. Then there was a crash of surf, a tumultuous banging overhead, on deck, and a heavy starboard roll. The man's weight came full on his wounded arm. He comforted himself with a noisy moan.

"Hush!" Ruiz clung to the porthole. "Good Heavens! We're putting about! Those savages are going to take the *Amistad* across the Atlantic Ocean! They're going to sail without charts. We'll be smashed on reefs! We'll split in a storm! We'll drown or starve to death in this hole!" The young man's voice rose to a scream. "Do you hear me?

We're sailing east—to be smashed on jutting reefs or eaten by the savages."

Montez listened with a curious unconcern. He would be dead from loss of blood before any other disaster could touch him. It is true that the blacks had by some miracle managed to turn the boat. They were headed straight for the open Atlantic, but what did one direction or another matter when death was close in any case?

The bleeding of the arm had ceased for the moment. Though he had no confidence in his recovery, nevertheless he tore a piece of the bed sheet and made a loose bandage. Then he crossed himself, gave himself up to his Maker, and lay down to wait for death.

The ship was going smoothly ahead now, and it was very comfortable in the bunk. After a little while Montez thought he might as well have a cigar while waiting for death to overtake him. He felt around in his coat pocket and found one. The sulphur matches were in reach, too, for a light.

Ruiz was noisily pacing the narrow space of the floor. Montez closed his eyes and wished for a little silence. The cigar tasted very good for so early in the morning. Or was it the night before? What a disastrous night! No one in Puerto Principe would

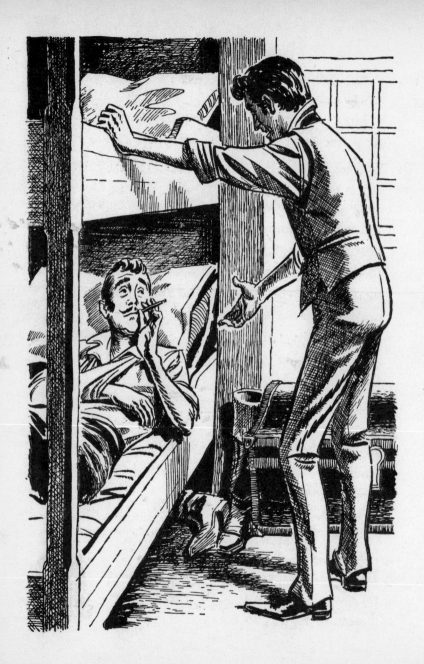

believe the story of that night. Perhaps it would be more desirable not to die of this wound after all, but to live to write an account of his sufferings. . . .

Cinque steered with both hands, as if by his firm grasp on the sun-baked wheel he could urge the ship forward. Only occasionally did he remove one hand to pull the red cloth, tunicwise over his left shoulder.

The four leaders, Tua, Fulway, Grabeau, and himself—all had these red-checkered tunics. Paramount chiefs always wore plenty of cloth, so it was right that the leaders on this voyage should have the biggest pieces that Antonio could find.

Everyone had something fine and new with which to adorn himself on this day of freedom. From the hold of the ship had come shawls to be made into turbans, feathers, trinkets, a necklace of brass rings, an embroidered waistcoat, and colored cloth of varying sizes.

Fulway had discovered these things and many more packed in barrels and boxes in the hold of the ship. That was when he was searching for palm oil for their morning meal. He had found rice and meat and huge amounts of salt for cooking, but no palm oil. He had looked thoroughly. It was unbelievable that rich men, to whom salt seemed no luxury, would lack a little palm oil to pour over the bowls of rice. But it was so.

The ways of the white men were past understanding. Nevertheless the things that they carried in the ship proved to have their uses. Something more than a loincloth is needed to give dignity and pride to a man.

The articles had been brought on the deck and palaver held in the matter of dividing them. At the same time the ship's company was organized into some sort of government, and four leaders were chosen.

Cinque was first in command, as in all other things. He was a young man, without even the dignity of a beard, but it was he who had brought them this freedom. After him came Grabeau, because he had seen boats and could handle ropes and sails. Tua, unable yet to walk or move about, was looked to for his great knowledge. Fulway was in charge of supplies and the water cask.

With Cinque, Fulway had numbered off the days their journey must take, remembering back across the weeks on the *Tecora*. Twice the new moon had been visible on that other vessel. Once, when they were still in African waters, the captives had seen the new moon in its familiar spot in the heavens, and again in midocean they had caught a glimpse of it. So they knew that the distance covered two moons or a little more than two moons.

Thirty or forty risings of the sun, Cinque thought, would be needed for their return, and Fulway organized and measured the supplies accordingly. And the ship's prow must always be pointed, as now, to the morning sun.

Cinque stood at the wheel of the boat. The sails were filled out and backed against the mast, and the wind and waves together made a sound like thunder or like the beating of many drums. As the drumbeats in a song do not make the melody, so the slashing of the wind against the canvas was but the accompaniment to Cinque's thoughts.

The first day of freedom was a fine, clear day, bright with the life-giving sun. When the sun comes to the edge of the world, a gate opens and the handmaidens of the sun cry out, "Make way for the king, the shining one!" And the sun walks across the sky—that sun who is king of light, the eye of the world.

Cinque held his body out to the sun, welcoming the sun's heat on every part of his body. The half-hundred days of darkness in the dank, sunless hold of the slave ship, in the wall-shadowed barracoon, burned itself out of Cinque's limbs. The sun swept the dark thoughts from his mind as well, until the words that came to his lips were no longer concerned with the hours of slavery.

He began to remember other things. He remembered his house and his wife in the moment when she came from the woman's quarters bringing his first-born, his son. What a fine, healthy boy that was! He recalled the planting season in all its stages, from the burning of the bush to the ripening rice and casava.

"I was going to open a new field for planting, a new field to feed my new-born son. I was thinking, 'We will name the boy Faah, the Waterbuck.' This I was thinking, when those kidnapers came up from behind. Now the harvest time is over and the ground is ripe for a new planting. What name has my child? My first-born?"

Suddenly, with his hands firm on the wheel, the young man raised his voice in a melody with which all his companions were familiar:

> Go ye ahead upon the way.
> Tell them we are coming,
> Like bright lizards running.

The singing man, Gnakowki, took up the song

and carried the rhythm. But the words came halt-
ingly, because he was not a Mandi like Cinque and
the others, but a Masai. He had only learned the
Mandingo language after capture. He was a stranger, but the only singing man among them. It is not
a profession to be picked up in a moment.

> Go ye ahead upon the way.
> Tell them we are coming,
> Like bright lizards running.

A chorus of voices took up the song. Men who
had spoken only of large impersonal things, like
the names of their rivers or mountains or of their
griefs, now began to remember other things. While
they were slaves they had seemed to exist without
a past. Now they rebuilt their lives out of small per-
sonal memories: out of nicknames, out of the number of goats they milked, out of the last hunt in the
forest. We-luwa was the first to sing a song of his
own:

> When I leave my hut and follow the leopard tracks,
> Men say, 'We will eat on the morrow,
> We-luwa is hunting.'
> I have killed five leopards and three elephants.
> I have a lion skin on the door of my hut.
> I am a hunter.

After We-luwa, each one sang his own verse and Gnakowki, the singing man, led the chorus, for how could he, a stranger, know the things they needed to remember?

A middle-aged man took up the song when We-luwa fell silent. His head was bald as a coconut shell, and smooth and brown. Over his shoulder he had knotted a purple cloth meant for the church at Puerto Principe. One ankle still bore the iron band, the mark of his captivity. The iron had cut so deep that Grabeau's file had not been able to remove it. The singer held his leg clumsily in front of him and blinked at the leg bar.

Kimbo sang of his home in the city of Mali, above the rapids of the Niger, and of his splendid house and many cattle. Ka-le, from his place high in the rigging, looked down at the little man curiously. He had not known Kimbo was a chief—not that it mattered greatly. Cinque was the leader now, and Grabeau the blacksmith, with his strong hands tugging at the ropes and calling to Ka-le to shift the rope lines.

"I have washed clothes in the Niger," Marga began shyly. It was not usual for a girl to join in making songs. But this was not a usual occasion. Ka-le was glad when Gnakowki gestured her to sing:

> Knee-deep in the water,
> Lifting the cloth up and down in the water,
> Or beating on a rock with a piece of wood,
> I saw on the bank a long spray of red flowers.
> When my brother saw me desire the flowers
> He climbed and tore it out of the tree.
> He gave it to me.

The brother, Fuli, had been taken captive with Marga. They had been brought down to the slave ship together and had been much comfort, one to the other, on the first journey, on the *Tecora*. The boy had died on that first ship. Marga would have liked to sing about her brother, but of course it was taboo to pronounce the name of the dead.

After Marga's verse was sung, Tua raised himself up on his elbows:

> Once when I was ill, my mother came to my pallet.
> She brought me milk. My mother.
> She had a round face, like the moon,
> With three marks on her forehead.
> Poor is the man
> Who has no mother to bring milk,
> No wife to grind corn.
> Go ye ahead upon the way.
> Tell them we are coming,
> Like bright lizards running.

Bau stepped forward, handsome in the waistcoat. He bowed to the singing man and to the company in general, and sang of his parents and the love they had shown him.

There was a stir overhead. Pugnaw was running up and down the topsail rigging:

> This is the way I will climb
> Coconut trees in my village.
> I will carry the knife between my teeth.
> If I meet a snake I will kill it.
> I will cut off the head of the snake
> As I cut the fruit of the coconut.
> I will climb the tallest tree in all the forest,
> So then my brothers will say I am a man.

One by one each of the others put his thoughts into words. Gnakowki was the last:

> To see the living earth again,
> What bright dreams!
> My fields, my rice fields!
> Go ye ahead upon the way.
> Tell them we are coming,
> Like bright lizards running.

The sun had been full in Cinque's face when the singing began. It was at his back before the last of the captives had had his say.

7. The Stars Are Strangers

THE *Amistad* headed her course fair to eastward, making good time, dead against the wind. But at sunset the wind died abruptly and the boat slowed down, drifting in the current. With darkness, the wind rose again, but it had shifted sharply to the south. Grabeau ordered the young boys aloft again to shift the sails one way and another.

There was much climbing and shouting and tugging at ropes, under the blacksmith's direction. Finally a quartering breeze caught the sails, and the schooner leaped forward in the water. But Cinque stood at the helm, puzzled and undecided.

Sky and sea were of one color—the color of smoke. There was no trace left of the sun. The stars were not yet visible. There was nothing to point the way in the trackless sea.

Antonio brought a lighted lamp and put it in its place in the square box riveted to the deck a few feet from the helm.

"What is that?" Cinque asked.

"The compass lamp. It is always my duty to light it at dark. How else could the captain see the way to steer?"

Cinque looked at the flaring lamp in the box. He called Grabeau and Fulway, and together they walked around it.

"A compass? What is that?" It was not a thing that had entered into their experience. "A white man's thing. It is not for us," said Fulway.

"I will not need it," Cinque answered. "I will be all right when the stars come out. There is after all no mistaking the four great stars that hang, on summer evenings, right at the gate of the sun. Over the third field—the one I planted to casava last year— that is where the four stars rise. I can keep the prow of the ship on the homeward path as soon as the four great stars come out."

"That is good," Fulway answered, "because we have scarcely food enough to last the journey. We cannot waste an hour."

"Yet it is no gain if we go in the wrong direction. The sea is very big." Cinque's hand was back on the wheel.

"There!" Fulway pointed to the sky where the evening star had come out in milky whiteness. "Is that your star?"

Cinque laughed. Fulway was plainly a city man. He did not know that you cannot find your way in the sky by one lone star. Nevertheless, as star after star appeared, now overhead, now to the right and left of the masts, the planter was distressed.

A red star set in a curve of stars hung on his left hand on the horizon. The constellation resembled the familiar Snake, but in this season that belonged high overhead.

His own four stars, which should rise over the gate of the sunrise, did not appear. The four stars that arranged themselves like the trunk of a palm tree across another palm tree, those guiding stars that he needed, were nowhere to be seen.

One constellation formed after another, their shapes unknown. These were not his stars. He was a stranger under this sky!

"The stars are not our stars. The sea is without a path. The wind fills the wings of the ship; the white man's ship cuts the empty water. But without knowledge of the direction we travel in vain, we cannot go on. . . . We must halt till sunrise," Cinque cried abruptly.

"If we stop the ship every night, it will take twice as long to make the journey." Fulway pointed to a water cask. "I have measured everything to the

least amount. Even with good fortune we will barely manage the journey. If bad luck delays us, if the stars are not our friends . . ." Fulway's gesture was heavy with despair.

"They are neither our friends nor our enemies; they are strangers, these stars," Cinque said. "How can the ship be brought to rest, Grabeau? Do you know a way?"

"We shall have to climb up and fold the sails, and throw out that heavy iron thing that has points to catch hold of the bottom of the sea."

"Lower sails, drop anchor, you fools," said Antonio under his breath.

Though he spoke so low, Cinque heard the boy. He sensed his contempt, too, for their lack of knowledge.

"The boy is right," he lamented. "We have taken the ship of the white men, but we are ignorant of its workings. Even those two prisoners down below know more than we do. We are as children or fools. Yet . . . do what must be done, Grabeau."

Montez and Ruiz, shut up in their cabin, heard the shouting and tramping overhead. Ruiz was pacing the cabin—five steps this way, three the other. He had been doing the same thing all day, like the pendulum of a wound-up clock or like some animal.

But Montez had not bothered to move. Except to light one cigar from another, he had scarcely stirred. To any plans for recovering the ship, to the hundred wild ideas Ruiz proposed, he made no reply at all.

Sunset came and then darkness in the stuffy cabin, and Ruiz continued to tramp the floor and to interpret every sound overhead to some hope of rescue.

Maybe the savages will quarrel among themselves. Maybe there will come a rescue ship. Maybe the crew went off for help. Maybe the schooner will drift back to land. Maybe, maybe, maybe . . .

Montez lay still and thought, "Must this talk go on?" Then came the clatter of anchor chains, and the rolling and pitching of the schooner gave place to the new sickening rhythm of a ship at rest.

Ruiz flung open the porthole. Nothing was to be seen except the lead-colored water and, on the horizon, the constellation Scorpio, rising.

"Mother of Heaven, what did you expect?" Montez laughed and pulled himself out of the bunk.

"What's so amusing?" Ruiz said. "They've hove to."

"Sure enough, they have lowered sail," Montez chuckled. "We are drifting—for the night, I imagine. That's the only thing they could do, under the circumstances."

"What's so all-fired amusing about that?" Ruiz repeated.

"It was crazy enough for them to try to sail a ship on the ocean without charts or knowledge of the use of the compass," the older man said. "If they really came from the African coast below the equator, then the course of the stars in our sky is unknown to them. They've had the shrewdness to find that out. Their good sense will be our good fortune, Pepé!"

Montez came to the porthole and stuck his head out. "Sure enough. We are drifting! Come, lend me a hand to get my boots off. I am going to sleep. Let us get some rest tonight. We will not sleep another night through on this foul ship again!"

The next morning, Antonio came to Cinque with a message. The ship had been under way again since sunrise. Cinque had spent the night in the captain's cabin, where he had carried Tua. He was back at the helm the moment the sun gave him a direction. There was a stiff wind and all sail was set.

The boat pitched forward with a great roar through the water.

Antonio had to shout against the wind. "The señores want speech with you."

Cinque pulled his red tunic closer over his shoulder. "If they come peaceably for a palaver, let them come," he answered.

Antonio looked puzzled. It was white men who had sent the message. When a white man spoke, then a black moved to obey—and quickly. Yet this African, this Bozal, stood and pulled his tunic about him and said, "Let them come if they would have palaver. . . ." It was not right! But the boy had no words to explain in Mandingo, so he carried the message back, softening it as best he could.

"Cinque cannot leave the helm," he called through the locked door. "At least he stands there as if the wheel and he were one—with that red cloak on. The cloak is nothing but a tablecloth, only he acts as if it were a cloak. But I know better. He said that you should come to him if you want to . . ."

"The devil he did." Ruiz' answer was exactly what Antonio had expected.

But Montez said, "Mother of Heaven, what is the difference?" He led the way up on the crowded, noisome deck, past the crates of chickens and the rice and raisins and fruit and water casks. He strode past the bodies of Komono and Ferrer, laid out under canvas, waiting for the day of burial.

"Two suns must rise and set before the burial." Antonio repeated what had been told him when he saw the white men swerve in disgust against the rail, away from the corpses.

"Have they got Ramon Ferrer laid out for a savage burial, too?" Ruiz muttered loudly.

"They meant well, señores." Antonio wanted trouble with neither side.

"Well, tell them to see that the deck is cleared by night of dead and living, too," Montez said, when they had come to the forecastle. "We'll sail their ship for them at night. That is what I wanted to say. But I don't want any blacks around . . . and no corpses. Make that clear."

In answer to Cinque's questions, Montez said surely he could guide the ship by the compass, at night, wherever desired.

There was a long talk between Cinque and Tua and Grabeau and Fulway. The rest of the men and boys gathered close until the narrow space around the helm was crowded.

Grabeau motioned the crowd away. He walked

around the compass box, studying the parts, the lamp, the glass, the moving, trembling finger.

"He wants to know," Antonio reported, "will the masters teach him to use the compass? He has seen ships before; he could learn, he says."

"We will sail the course at night. That's our offer." Montez answered with a rude businesslike tone meant to close the argument. "Tell them I know very well why they hove to and drifted through the night without getting anywhere. The stars are strangers to them. They are white men's stars and this is a white man's instrument. Tell them they will never get to Africa alive if they sail only in the day. Tell them the way is long and they will starve."

"I understand." Fulway gestured the others to be silent. "This instrument you sail with is a white man's. We will respect it."

"They are fools," Ruiz muttered.

"Mother of Heaven, what would you?" Montez turned to Antonio. "Tell them to leave bowls of food, a freshly cooked chicken, as long as those crates of fowls last. And tell them to get these bodies overboard and get themselves below and out of sight before sunset."

"So be it," Cinque answered. "We will sail by

day and the whites at night. When we get to the land of the sun, which is our land, we will set them ashore and treat them well. We forgive them. Let our differences be at an end."

Antonio had no way of knowing that this was the regular way to close a palaver between equals. He did not repeat the words or attempt to translate their meaning. Surely even Cinque must feel the difference between himself and the señores.

For all Señor Ruiz' unshaved face and crumpled clothes, for all the smell of the dried blood on Señor Montez' bandaged arm, these were white men. For all the others' fine bearing and grand looks, their skins were black. They were nothing. But Cinque did not seem to be aware of the difference.

That night again Cinque came into the cabin with Tua. They could see nothing on deck, but they could hear Montez at the wheel shouting directions to Ruiz and Antonio. Cinque spoke gratefully of the help offered.

"How good it is we did not kill unnecessarily. These men are our friends now! They will sail the night seas and we will come to our homes again. I will see my son, Tua."

Toward morning, while Cinque was asleep in the captain's bunk, Tua heard the men on deck strangely busy with the ropes. This puzzled him vaguely, for the wind had not changed.

Day followed day—the white men and the Africans met only at sunrise and sunset. When Ruiz passed the Negroes, he gave them black looks. For Cinque he had a special hatred. The savage seemed to have forgotten the barracoon where Ruiz had turned him this way and that on the slave block, and finally bought him for money.

When they passed each other on deck or in the gangway, instead of drawing back and lowering his face, the Negro held up his hand in greeting. The hand that had killed the white captain! And he looked straight ahead into the face of his master, with no shame. It was almost more than Ruiz could tolerate.

Montez had to calm Ruiz, reminding him of the stake in this game they were playing.

8. By Day and by Night

DAY followed day. The *Amistad* made her track through the trackless waters. At first, in the daytime, her course was uncertain and wavering, subject to the wind. But it was not long before the handling of the ship steadied under Grabeau's teaching.

Ka-le especially became skillful at reefing or letting out sail. He spent little time on the cluttered deck. Most of his waking hours were passed on the lookout or climbing in the rigging, high on the fore topsail mast. He was sure-footed and quick, and soon learned to tell one line from another, so that the puffing sails responded to his bidding.

"These cloths that catch the wind are a good thing," he said to Marga one day when they had climbed to the lookout together. "When I get home I will ask my sister to weave me a cloth. I will fasten it to my canoe. Then no one will be able to overtake me on the river."

The thought of weaving reminded him of his mother. He would have liked to speak of his mother's skill at making cloth. But he did not know—he thought he would never know—if his mother was in the land of the living. So he did not speak her name.

But the girl read Ka-le's silent thought. She sat quiet for a moment, in sympathy. Then she smiled and agreed that cloth to catch the wind was a wonderful thing.

But skillful as the Negroes became, there was a difference in the speed of the ship by day and by night. At night, Montez came to life, and the ship with him. The Spaniard was an experienced navigator. Though he had only Ruiz and Antonio for crew, he pushed the schooner to the utmost. All through the night the ship's prow cut a straight smooth path in the water. Only at dawn was there apt to be a wavering.

Tua slept badly. The gunshot wound throbbed with dull throbbing and kept him awake. Every morning he would listen to the noises above, on deck. He had no confidence in the white men. But as long as the stars were their stars, he could do nothing. So he remained silent, a thing for which he afterward blamed himself.

On the seventh day there was a storm .The ship rolled frightfully, dipping her yards into the water on each side. Fuli, one of the young men, climbed the ropes to help Ka-le get the sails lowered. In his haste he lost his balance and fell into the sea and was lost.

At the sound of the cries of those who saw Fuli drown, Montez came on deck. Since there was no guiding sun, he said that he would take the wheel. He ordered the Negroes below, and they obeyed. Cinque was very grateful to the white man. It was good to know that even in this storm the *Amistad* was pushing homeward.

The next day the sun came out and there was a new rejoicing. Gnakowki discovered a guitar in the forecastle, under one of the hammocks that had belonged to the sailors. It had the wrong number of strings and the tones were coarse, but at least it was an instrument for making music. His fingers plucked the strings with the pleasure of a hungry man who eats again.

> Go ye ahead upon the way.
> Tell them we are coming,
> Like bright lizards running.

But as day followed day without a glimpse of shore, the voyagers on the *Amistad* found out that there is such a thing as too much sun. The drinking water turned blackish and the corn moldy. The rice had long given out, and all such luxuries as meat or butter.

The confinement, the lack of good food, and the unchanging sunlight joined together and brought on a fever. Sickness went through the ship like fire through a parched field. Five boys and men died, four in one day. They were mourned, not as strangers mourned by strangers—they had become known to each other. They had homes, they had a country to which they were returning. It was very sad to die so near the end of the voyage.

So sang Gnakowki in a mourning song, thinking surely the voyage could not last much longer—there could not be much more of the endless sweep of water.

Gnakowki's song woke a violent hope in the voyagers. When they came from below in the morning, they rushed from one side of the ship to the other, saying, "Has it come in the night? Is our land visible?"

When the sun set on empty sea, on the wide circle of nothingness, they lay down saying, "It will surely come in the night."

The schooner meanwhile presented a pitiable

sight. The top part of the foremast had snapped off in the storm, like a palm tree in the woods. Ruiz would lean against the stump and entertain himself half the night, listing the ship's shortcomings.

"Look at her," he would say, fascinated. "Paint on her side puffed out and cracked. Sails torn . . . stern piece encrusted with barnacles. Every time she rises on a sea I'll bet she shows her copper, torn like wastepaper. We ought to pound her rust off," he'd say, and then, pendulumlike, his mind would swing away from that idea. The wilder the *Amistad*'s looks became, the more chance there'd be of gaining attention of any passing ship.

Now that they had come to the open sea, that was Ruiz' great hope: the dream of rescue. Once or twice on deck in the night they even glimpsed a ship's light, like some misplaced star on the distant horizon.

On a clear, sunny afternoon, there came bearing down on the *Amistad* a beautiful sight: a vessel in full sail, leaning over to the breeze. Sailors could be seen grouped on the forecastle, the cook leaning out of the cook house. The captain shouted through a speaking trumpet. There was a flag with red stripes on it—an American flag.

Through the porthole in the cabin Ruiz saw the

vessel. Montez had to stop him forcibly from rushing out to demand that the Negroes draw alongside. The most Ruiz could do was to tie a rag on a stick and fly it as a signal of distress out of the porthole. But the vessel shifted its course to the leeward side, and the signal went unheeded.

Another time Ka-le, on the lookout, sighted a small fishing sloop. When the sloop hove in hailing distance, Fulway put a small boat down and, taking Antonio with him, went to bargain for meat and fresh water. As it turned out, Antonio's Spanish was as useless as Fulway's own native language. But the coins that Cinque provided from the captain's chest served instead of spoken language.

Ruiz, this time, broke loose from Montez' clutches and ran up the hatchway shouting hysterically. However, the fishermen pulled away with great promptness after the bargaining was finished. It was not every day that you could exchange a cask of water and a side of salt pork for ten gold dollars!

Grabeau watched the sloop go over the horizon. "When I first saw people on a boat like that in Lomboko," he said, "I thought the ship was their home, that they knew no other. I picked up a piece of earth to show them, as if they had never seen the earth. They laughed to find so simple a person, one who believed that human creatures could make a home on the sea."

"Now," he said bitterly, "I think we will be that new kind of people, living on this ship, never to see the land again."

"I dreamed, but I was not aware that I was dreaming," Cinque said to Tua one morning before daybreak in the cabin. "I stood by a small river, and there was a single tree trunk forming a bridge; but when I tried to cross it, a chameleon ran in my path. I do not care for the chameleon; he is a death bringer. Yet I crossed. This I know, because I could see myself on the other side as well. I walked up a small hill with one banana tree growing on it. I wanted a banana for my son."

"You are lucky to dream," Tua responded. "Since I had those irons on, I have had no dreams. Even my spirit is not free to wander."

"But soon, very soon, dear Tua, you will see the living earth again. Already we have passed the second moon," Cinque answered.

"Even the moon," said Tua, "is not in its proper place in the heavens."

The food bought from the fishing boat lasted only a few days. Then there was only corn meal and biscuits covered with a green mold, and few in number. Fulway counted them with despairing eyes.

Faguina failed to wake up one morning. The body of the little man, who had been a slave even in the Mandi country, was discovered by Fulway. He could not help a sigh of relief that there was one less to feed from that day onward. But he spared a little of his own biscuit to put in Faguina's burial bowl.

It was on this same day that Ka-le caught the land bird. He saw a flock winging its way across the masthead and went up the rigging, hand over hand, foot after foot. Coming to the crossbeam he stretched out his hand and brought down a bird.

"A land bird!" There was a shout of fierce delight. The small brown creature was passed from hand to hand as if it were something miraculous. Then Ferni asked what was the name of the bird, saying she had never seen one of just such color and markings, and with the bill shaped so. The voyagers looked at one another, and true happiness passed out of their faces. A land bird surely, but not from their own land!

It was noticed now that the flock was going away from the sun, not toward it. The birds were even as the stars were—not theirs. A silence swept

over the ship as they ceased to watch the flock
of strange birds overhead. They turned to Cinque
with one unspoken question.

There was usually a rhythm and serenity in
Cinque's movements which spread confidence.
When he lifted his face and looked about him, people ceased to fret and were at peace. This was the
effect Cinque had on those around him. But now
darkness settled on his face. His hands left the
wheel. His arms hung loose at his side, his head
dropped between his shoulders.

After a while he lifted his head again, as if he
had pushed some thought away from him, as if it
were too great a burden.

"What is one bird?" asked Cinque, when night
had come and he had retired with Tua to the cabin.

But Tua remembered the noises of the white
men at the helm in the early daylight. Remembered? The thing had never, throughout the voyage, been really far from his mind. It lay just be-
neath his waking thought, a constant troubling burden. Now, at last, it was clear enough. The course
the white man sailed in the night was not their
course! As the stars and the birds were strangers,
so would the land be.

9. Land

Tua did not sleep at all. After the early hours of the night had passed, he crept outdoors, moving quietly. Keeping out of sight of the white men, he made his way to the afterdeck. He stood there by the rail, straining his eyes for the thing he feared to find.

Before dawn, a light appeared. Tua stared, wordless. It was not a fire and it was not a star, just a cold unnatural light above the water.

The sky turned gray and the stars disappeared— the hateful stars. But the light remained. It rose high on a bald shaft, a thing of stone such as men must have built. Several vessels outlined themselves here and there on the horizon—tugs, merchantmen, fishing sloops.

Tua gave them no more than a glance. His eyes were fastened on the blue line of visible shore. The light grew, and the land took on different colors:

brown sand, green, wind-blown trees, the towering lighthouse raised on a cliff. And beyond the cliff smoke curled up, a sign of human habitation.

The boom swung violently about. There was a sudden shout, immediately cut short. But there was no mistaking the triumph in that cry. To Tua, all was plain.

Ruiz and Antonio were up in the rigging. Now Ruiz joined the older man at the helm. Again came that cry of triumph. Ruiz could not restrain himself.

Would it be better now to kill at once? Tua considered. To be rid of the tricksters, raise the alarm, sail out of this place on the sea again?

But they had no water, no food, no one to pilot the ship in unknown paths. Tua's wound throbbed, and he pushed against his belly to stop the pain. But his heart throbbed too, and tears were rolling down his cheeks.

In all the time of their captivity he had taken pride in his self-control, saying, "Let the women, let the children cry. I will not weep, because I am a man." But now it was pleasant to shut out the sight of that alien land with tears.

After awhile he became aware of someone behind him, the harsh sound of breathing in his ear

Even as Tua turned, Cinque dropped his red tunic to the deck and leaped to the rail and dived. His body cut the water with such clean swiftness that it made no sound. Tua swung out with his long arms to stop Cinque, seizing on nothingness.

He started to call, then checked himself with a glance toward the forecastle. He couldn't tell whether or not the white men had caught sight of the swimmer. He could see them tugging at the ropes, lowering sail. They acted as if they thought themselves alone on the deck.

Why had Cinque gone? What was in his mind? He was swimming toward the land with long purposeful strokes, going for help perhaps. Without a new supply of food and water they could not get themselves out of this trap. But how could Cinque make known his needs? What sort of human beings would he find on that alien coast? How could he speak? How make himself understood?

"Cinque!" Tua called softly.

The figure in the water did not pause or change course.

Light footsteps sounded in the hatchway. Ka-le came noiselessly to Tua's side. "Land! We've come to land!" the boy whispered, clutching Tua's arm.

Tua gestured despairingly toward the bow of

the ship. "Land of *their* choosing," he answered. "We've been tricked, don't you understand? The white men turned back the wheel in the night. Every night they changed the course of the ship. All the days' journeying, all the toilsome sail to the sun was undone in the night. Now Cinque is making for that land to which the whites have brought us."

"Cinque?"

Tua pointed to the ripples in the water, to the dark head and arms of the swimmer, halfway between the ship and the shore.

"What is he doing?" Ka-le's voice trembled.

Tua shook his head. "I don't know. It was a crazy thing to go off alone without weapons, without the gift of speech, without even the clothes of a leader." He pointed to the tunic crumpled on the deck. "Cinque will be killed or, worse still, enslaved. That land is inhabited. There's the roof of a house and smoke coming from the roof hole."

"And people!" Ka-le's keen eyes had caught a glimpse of two men walking down a path to the rocky beach. They were darkly clothed men, not in themselves frightening except for one thing: their faces were white-skinned. "White men," the boy whispered.

Ka-le's hopeless tone seemed to rouse Tua from his own despair. "I have heard," he said suddenly, "that not all white men make slaves of our people. There are lands where white and black live peacefully one with the other. At least I have heard so. I know a word in the language of those people. The word is *free*. It means 'no enslavement.'"

The boy looked at the shore, where the two soberly dressed men moved steadily closer. The green grassy slope and sandy shore seemed somehow less hateful than before. What if indeed the ship had come to such a place as Tua described; a free land?

Then the brief glimmer of hope flickered out. The traitors at the helm would not have guided the *Amistad* to such a place. Unless . . . unless they lacked Tua's knowledge!

"Does Cinque know this word free?" Ka-le spoke urgently. He saw that the swimmer was not far from shore now, in shallow water.

Before Tua could answer there was movement behind them. Grabeau and Fulway came running from aft. There was fury in their eyes.

Grabeau wasted no words. "There is land on this side, too!" he said to Fulway. Then he came to the rail and leaned close to Tua. "We are trapped," he whispered. "Those two at the wheel—they must be killed. Where's Cinque? Surely now he will see we must kill them!"

For answer, Tua pointed shoreward. Cinque was standing now, walking in the shallow water. The watchers at the rail could see his arm raised in greeting to the strangers on the beach.

"They are white men. He will be captured!" Fulway said. "Cinque must not go to meet them alone!"

He tore at his garment, everything else forgotten. The traitorous masters could be taken care of later. It was Cinque who mattered now. Cinque must be saved. Fulway leaped to the rail, a knife between his teeth. He stood poised for diving.

But Grabeau held him back. "Not that way!" he cried. "Take the small boat. Tua cannot swim with his wound. Tua has the gift of language. We must have Tua with us."

At mention of the small boat, Ka-le turned and raced amidships. Other men came up the hatchway, helped him untie the ropes, and push the boat overside.

In the excitement of launching the rowboat, no one noticed Montez and Ruiz. No one saw them slip away from the forecastle deck and dart down the passageway to their cabin. No one paid any attention to Antonio, rigid in the rigging, watching the scene with eyes bright as a tiger's on a dark night.

Ka-le only stopped long enough to catch up Cinque's discarded tunic, then went nimbly overside. Grabeau threw him the oars and followed. Together they fitted the oars in the oar locks. Then they rowed to the spot directly below, where Tua stood by the rail. Fulway had disappeared; but now he returned up the hatchway, lugging the box of coins from the captain's cabin.

Tua climbed painfully down. A jutting timber, a rope dangling almost to the water, and then Grabeau's upstretched arms helped him. The barnacles cut sharp as knives. His legs and thighs were scratched and bleeding. But he did not notice.

The attention of those in the boat, as of the others who crowded against the rail, was on the shore. Cinque was striding forward toward the strangers, toward the white men. Cinque moved slowly, with great dignity. His arm, dripping with water, was raised in greeting.

The unknown men had stopped short. They drew no weapons. But one never knew. Perhaps this waiting was another white man's trick.

"Cinque!" This time Tua shouted. But there was no sign that his voice had carried to the shore.

Cinque and the unknowns were no more than six paces apart when the boat at last scraped the sand bar. "Cinque!" Tua called again.

This time his shout attracted attention. With a jerk of their heads, the two white men turned to stare at the new arrivals, and Cinque showed by a gesture that he too was aware of the happenings behind him. But he kept his eyes fastened on the bearded face of the older man, on the pale eyes of the young one.

Were they alarmed? Would they produce fire-arms, white men's weapons, that might be hidden in their clothing? Cinque kept his own hands raised, palms out. He kept his eyes steady and calm. By the sound of footsteps he knew that his friends were quite close now. Still there was no unfriendly move on the part of the natives of this land. There was no fright in their faces, only surprise and a great wonder.

"We come in peace," Cinque said slowly, in his own tongue.

"What in tarnation!" the older man said under his breath. To Cinque, though the words meant nothing, the tone betrayed a not-understanding.

Tua stepped forward until he was at Cinque's elbow. Perhaps the language of the Arabs was known to these strangers. Almost every traveler Tua had seen in his lifetime knew the Arabian greeting, "Peace be with you." But when Tua stretched out his palms and said, "Salaam Aleikum," the white men looked as puzzled as before.

"We must be far from home indeed," Tua whispered sadly, "if the language of the Arabs is unknown."

Ka-le tugged at Tua's tunic. "Try that other language, that word *free*."

It was not the custom for a young boy, not yet grown, to advise his elders, but Tua followed Ka-le's advice. With a gesture that included the earth on which they stood, the strangers, and themselves, Tua questioningly spoke the word: *free*.

The older man nudged his companion. "Sounds like they're asking, is this free soil they're standing on?" he exclaimed. "I guess, being black, they're afraid of slavers."

The young man nodded. "It could be." He nodded his head and repeated Tua's gesture. "This is free land. Slavery hasn't been lawful in the state of New York for fifty years."

The man's nod, the look on the white man's face, was enough for the Africans. Grabeau opened his hand and let his knife fall.

Fulway said, "It is good. We can palaver. But first, Cinque, you should get some garments on. How else will they know you're an important man? Besides, I brought the box of metal pieces."

Fulway set the box of coins at Cinque's feet while Grabeau and Ka-le placed the tunic, one end forward, over Cinque's left shoulder. But even the red tunic did not seem enough. A great man, a paramount chief, wears plenty of cloth and adornments.

Grabeau took off his turban of purple silk and wound it on Cinque's forehead. Ka-le snatched off his necklace of brass rings and passed it to Cinque. Not to be outdone, Fulway added his new charm on its leather thong. Then they stepped back a few paces, leaving an appropriately clothed leader to palaver with the strangers.

The white men had watched with interest. "I get it," the younger man murmured. "They're trying to say that the one who swam ashore is the head man. Well, even without his trappings he looked like a leader."

"The blacks are like Indians, I reckon," the old

man agreed. "Indians set great store on dress and other ceremonies."

"He's trying to say something more," the young man answered.

Cinque had put his hand to his chest and spoken his name. He repeated it several times.

"Cinque?" the young, pale-eyed man caught on. "Your name is Cinque? Mine's Ellis, Graham Ellis, and his is Captain Green."

Cinque nodded and motioned toward each of his companions in turn, speaking their names. Then he pointed to the ship, to show how the voyagers had come.

This was unnecessary. There was not a man, woman, or child on the Atlantic seacoast who had not been on the watch for the mysterious long black schooner. The *Amistad* had zigzagged in the coastal waters for the last month.

But even before that the captain of the Merchantman *Evalina* had brought report of the amazing ship. He had sighted it sailing due east off the Carolinas, early in July.

"I ran within a few yards," the captain had reported in a Charleston newspaper, "saw only blacks on board, a black man at the wheel. One of the blacks had a knife in his hand, which he flourished over his head, making signals to the *Evalina* to keep on. The Schooner's name was the *Amistad*. A top-sail yard was gone. Bottom very foul."

Then certain Maryland fishermen had boasted of trading with some mysterious Negroes, and showed Spanish coins to prove it. The newspapers had printed that tale up and down the coast. After that, the papers hardly let a day go by without printing some report from a sea captain who had sighted the *Amistad* on its crazy course. Some called it a pirate vessel. Some called it a ghost ship. Others called it the mutiny ship and gave it a wide berth on the sea.

At first, being a retired seaman himself, Green had laughed at the stories. But only yesterday, August 25 that was, the *Sag Harbor Gazette*, right here on Long Island, had printed a report from Sandy Hook, New Jersey. The suspicious long black schooner had been sighted in the night, headed north.

Graham Ellis was equally well informed, though his news was gathered from the New Haven papers. At Yale University, where he was a tutor, the mysterious vessel was a favorite subject of dinner conversation. Ellis himself had been of the belief that the *Amistad* did not exist at all. Now he was face to face with five black men who seemed to know only one word of English and that word: *free*.

There was a pause. The Negroes seemed to be trying to consider how to go on. There was whispered talk between them. Then the boy and the tall, lean-faced man, came forward and carried the box they'd brought and placed it at Captain Green's feet. They opened the box with a flourish and revealed a pile of money.

"Tarnation!" Green muttered. "There must be two or three hundred dollars there. Where do you reckon it came from, Graham? What do they want to trade it for?"

The answer to that last question took time and patience. The sun, to which Cinque pointed repeatedly, was high in the sky before Green and Ellis felt they had the thing clear. These Negroes evidently wanted to sail that ship of theirs east, to Africa. They wanted supplies and a navigator. They'd give the money and the ship too, once they'd come to the end of their journey, to anybody who'd take up their offer.

It looked like good business to Captain Green. The Long Islander was not rightly a captain. In his sailing days he had never risen beyond first mate. He had somehow become known as Captain Green

after he had quit the sea. But captain or not, he knew sailships; and, with a little fixing, the *Amistad* looked seaworthy.

Green didn't ask questions as to how the ship came into the possession of the Africans. They couldn't talk English, and the less he knew the better. He looked on this as strictly a business matter, and he laughed at the younger man for the admiring gaze Ellis fastened on Cinque.

"You're like all the New Englanders," he said, "full of notions about the blacks. If you don't watch out, you'll be joining the abolitionists. Don't you forget," Green said sourly, "your pa made money as a slaver."

Graham Ellis flushed. It was true that he was the son of a shipowner who had made several voyages to Africa. But he was also the son of a Quaker mother who had persuaded her husband to give up the trade in human beings. The young man rather bitterly thought of himself as the product of the America of his time, half slave and half free.

Graham was not an abolitionist, but it made him ashamed to hear abolitionists, like Garrison and Tappan and Lydia Childs, laughed at. Lydia Childs was a Quaker, too. Perhaps if his mother were alive she would be taunted with being an abolitionist and a friend of the Negro.

The young man stared at the symbols Cinque was drawing with a stick in the sand. How clear, how steady this black man's purpose! And Captain Green was following the drawing with an understanding eye. For whatever reasons, the captain was going to be helpful to these people. That was more than the abolitionists, for all their talk, seemed to accomplish. Ellis didn't know what to believe.

Suddenly Green stood up and hoisted the money box onto his shoulders. "Come along around the point," he said, with broad gestures. "There's another man, Pelatiah Fulham, you'd better include in this bargain. When the time comes I can sail it, but that ship of yours is going to need some repairs."

The people left on the ship had not moved from the rail. They saw their leaders follow the strangers peacefully and confidently around the point of land. In spite of all, it appeared things were going to end well.

Gnakowki beat out a song, and the three girls went down to the cook's galley to scrape up the last of the corn meal to prepare some food.

The watchers saw a trim gray ship, flying a flag of red and white stripes, cruising around the *Amistad.* They watched calmly as small boats were launched. The Negroes on deck were not suspicious. They thought that Cinque had sent help. They accepted the arrival of the small boats without alarm.

It was not until the white men, Montez and Ruiz, rushed from below with glad cries and tears of joy that the people saw their danger. Then it was too late to put up a fight. They were driven, at gun point, down the passageway to the space in back of the galley.

"What did you expect?" Antonio shouted as they stumbled into the dark space and the door was barred. He was sure now which side he was on. He listened to the señores telling a tale of mutiny and murder to those Americans from the Coast Guard Cutter. And he felt more comfortable than he had at any time since the death of Captain Ferrer.

Cinque and the rest of them had almost fooled him, with their talk about it being right to go to their homeland. But now he knew better! White was white and black was black, as it should be. And the men with guns were going to shore to bring Cinque and the others back in chains.

10. Was It Mutiny?

I simply don't believe it!" Ellis Graham leaned forward in his chair in the dining hall at Yale. "I've seen the man they call a murderer, I tell you. I've seen and talked with Cinque—as much as you can talk with somebody who doesn't speak your language. There's something wrong with the story those Spaniards tell."

The young tutor sat at the head of one of the dining tables. The clatter of dishes and scraping of benches at other tables in the dining hall forced him to raise his voice.

The evening meal was over, and most of the scholars and their tutors were leaving. But the boys at Graham Ellis' table were deep in talk about the prisoners who had been brought to New Haven that day. They did not stir.

A rare sight it had been, in the forenoon, to see forty savages clanking their chains across the Green to the prison house. One of the mutineers, the one charged with the murder of the captain of the *Amistad,* had chains on both arms and legs.

A fat boy, sitting at the tutor's right, laughed. He said, "I reckon there's no mistake, sir. The Spaniards tell a pretty straightforward story of mutiny and murder. It seems they were transporting their slaves from one end of Cuba to another, and the blacks mutinied and killed the captain and crew and seized the ship. They would have gotten away with it if the owners—name of Ruiz and Montez, very pleasant fellows—hadn't played a smart trick.

"It seems the Africans sailed east in the daytime and the Spaniards changed the course of the ship every night. For two months they've been zigzagging out in the ocean."

Another boy, Gil Johnson, spoke up in a southern drawl. "I hear Gedney, commander of the rescue ship, has put in for salvage money. I wish I were in his shoes! What with rescuing the ship and the shipload of slaves and other property he'll collect a neat reward."

A laugh went around the table. Gil Johnson spent his allowance the first week of every month and then borrowed from his friends until the next money arrived from Virginia. Graham Ellis didn't join in the laughter. He was still trying to make sense of the events he had witnessed on the beach at Culloden Point.

The Africans had about completed their bargain with Pelitiah Fulham and Captain Green. They had arranged to bring the *Amistad* around the point, to the ocean side of Long Island. There the mast would be mended, new sails provided, and the ship stocked with food and water. In three days, Green had promised, the ship would be ready to continue its voyage. He and Fulham would go as navigators, and at the end of the voyage, the money and the ship would be theirs.

Everything had been peaceful and friendly, until suddenly the beach was overrun with Navy men. The Negroes had been clubbed and dragged into the lifeboat of the cutter. The commander, Gedney, had thrown the money box in the bottom of the boat and pushed off, leaving Ellis and his friends speechless with surprise.

"There's one lot of money Gedney won't collect," Graham said, pushing his plate away and planting his elbows on the dining table. "When the sailors hauled the captives back to their ship, I followed in a painter. I left Green and Fulham on the beach thanking their lucky stars they'd been warned off from murderers. But I couldn't make sense out of what was happening—couldn't then and can't now."

"What about the money?" Gil asked.

Graham smiled faintly. "When they got to deep water at the end of Culloden Point, Cinque rose up and lifted the coin chest in his chained arms. Before the sailors could stop him, he flung the thing overboard. The money that was going to buy their way home is at the bottom of the ocean."

Enoch Hopkins, at the end of the long table, came around to stand in back of Graham Ellis' chair. Enoch was a farm boy whose home was not far from New Haven. As a rule he was very quiet—good in his studies, but not much of a mixer with the other scholars.

His face was flushed now, and he spoke eagerly. "Mr. Ellis, maybe they're not lawfully slaves at all. They can't be if they're fresh out of Africa. Spain's got a treaty with England that says slaves can't be imported anymore."

The tutor nodded gratefully. "That's what I'm trying to say," he answered. "My guess is that those people over in the prison house are natives of Africa who were kidnaped from their homes. Heaven knows how, they thought they had found a way to return."

"They're mutineers and murderers," Gil Johnson murmured under his breath.

If Enoch or Graham Ellis heard, they did not bother to answer.

"How can the truth be discovered?" Enoch asked. "How can the Africans even tell their side of the story?"

"They speak a language like nothing I ever heard," Graham responded. "There's a boy, no older than you—about as tall, but thin and bony. He kept repeating one word of English, just one word: *free*. And there was an old man who had an open wound in his stomach. He tried to say something in what sounded like Arabic. Only I don't know any Arabic. But the leader, Cinque, got along with sign language and drawing in the sand."

"Wanting to get food and water and somebody to pilot a ship," Enoch said slowly. "Those are easy to explain. Enslavement isn't."

"Exactly," the tutor agreed. "These Africans haven't even the knowledge of our laws. They're defenseless, tongueless."

"But you said one of them seemed to know Arabic, sir," Enoch urged. He pushed back a lock of hair that had fallen across his forehead. He was always doing that in class when he was interested or excited by an idea. "Gibbs! Old Gibbs knows Arabic."

"Professor Gibbs?" Ellis smiled. Willard Gibbs

wasn't old, except in the eyes of this sixteen-year-old student.

"Professor Gibbs," Enoch explained. "He teaches ancient languages. You're so taken with your rocks and earth, Mr. Ellis, you don't notice what other people are teaching. Gibbs is the same way. He doesn't think we ought to study anything but words —'sacred symbols of human thought' he calls 'em."

Graham Ellis stood up abruptly. "Excuse us, gentlemen!" he said and looked around at the empty table. He had been so deep in talk with the one boy who understood the problem that he hadn't noticed the others when they quietly left the table. Now he took Enoch by the elbow and started without ceremony for the door.

"Are we going to see Gibbs now? Right off?" Enoch asked, matching his stride to the tutor's.

"We are," Graham Ellis said. "There's no time to lose with the Spaniards clamoring for their property and Gedney for his salvage money. The Negroes will be on their way back to Cuba before anybody finds out whether they're legally slaves or free men."

Early next morning Ka-le stood at the barred window of the New Haven prison. Behind him, the *Amistad* captives. Their chains had been re-huddled in hopeless attitudes, were about half of moved. They were free to wander around the cell, but they hardly stirred from the places where they had thrown themselves the night before.

There were, in the prison house, four rooms that served as cells. Most of the prisoners had been crowded into two of the rooms. The girls had been placed alone in a third room, and Cinque, still in chains, was in solitary confinement. His friends had seen him being marched off, heavily chained. They did not know whether he was still living. They had not been able to speak to him since they were parted in that first prison house, on the seacoast.

Ka-le stood at the window looking out on the green grass and the wind blowing through the trees. He was thinking that Cinque did not even know that Tua was dead. Ka-le did not shrink from naming Tua, the gentle one, in his thoughts. He would not mind if Tua's spirit should return and come asking. Tua had been good and wise, even if he had been mistaken in that word in the white man's language, that word *free*.

"I will speak Tua's name even though he has died," the boy thought bitterly. "But I will not speak that word *free* again."

Ka-le was still staring out of the window when Ellis Graham came across the Green with two other

white men. One was bearded and stoop-shoul-
dered, the other seemed but a boy. Ka-le clenched
his hands. He felt no friendship for the man from
the beach. Meeting him had brought such hope,
and then he had stood by while hope was taken
away.

There was a grating sound. The door to the cell
opened and the jailer brought the three inside.
Ka-le watched without moving while Graham Ellis
searched for a familiar face in the room.

"Ka-le," Ellis said. Ka-le came slowly forward,
but he did not smile or raise his hand in greeting.
He came as to a total stranger.

Ellis pointed to the white boy by his side, a boy
with eyes the color of indigo, and dressed in awkward, heavy garments. "Enoch Hopkins," Ellis said,
"and Willard Gibbs." He repeated Gibbs' name
twice, to give it importance. His eyes traveled over
the silent room, seeking Cinque and the man Tua,
the sick one, who spoke what might be Arabic.

Not seeing them, he turned to Mr. Pendleton,
the marshal and jailkeeper, and asked a question.

"Cinque?" the jailer showed surprise. "He's a
dangerous murderer. I've got him downstairs in
solitary. But I'll bring him up if you'll take the responsibility. I don't know about any sick man;

this is all there is in these two rooms. Except the little girls. My wife is fitting them with some decent dresses. I'll fetch 'em in when she's clothed 'em proper."

The man unlocked a connecting door and disclosed another room full of captives. Then he went away, barring the door behind him.

While he waited, Graham Ellis moved from one silent group to another. Mr. Pendleton had said that none were missing except Cinque and some girls. Yet he did not find the sick man who had spoken words in Arabic.

The door opened once more, and Marga, Ferni, and Teme slipped in, robed from neck to ankle in stiff calico wrappers. They looked unhappy in the ugly garments. They did not leave the doorway.

No one spoke.

Outside the closed door the clanking of chains, the grating of a lock, the creaking of a door, sounded strangely loud in the silence. The door opened and Cinque stood erect on the threshold.

With cries of joy, the captives crowded around him. Cinque was still alive. He was with them again!

Cinque caught sight of Graham Ellis. He moved toward him as to an old friend, hand upraised, eyes calm and confident.

Ka-le sighed in relief. He had been wrong to doubt these men and this boy. They came in friendship. He caught Enoch's eye and smiled.

Again Ellis spoke the names of Willard Gibbs and Enoch Hopkins. Then he spoke Tua's name, questioningly.

At mention of Tua's name, there was a vague troubled stir in the room. The three girls, who had been hovering close to Cinque, slid down at his feet and dropped their heads.

"We wanted to see Tua," Ellis explained, "because he gave a greeting which sounded like 'Salaam Aleikum.' These are words of a language Professor Gibbs can speak. Gibbs thought maybe he could talk with Tua, could help you."

As Ellis spoke, Cinque's eyes traveled to the anxious faces of his companions. He saw that they were frightened and sad at every mention of Tua's name. He knew then that Tua had died.

Professor Gibbs nudged Ellis. "I am afraid we are too late to speak to the man you seek. From the look on their faces, he is evidently no longer living."

"Must have died in New London then," the jailer said. "These you see were all that were handed over to my keeping. And a scared bunch they are, all but that one charged with murder."

"Professor Gibbs!" Enoch Hopkins said. "Isn't

134

there any way to speak to them? You know so many languages!"

Willard Gibbs sighed. "Arabic seemed a real hope," he answered. "But I don't know a single African tongue, and if I did it wouldn't be likely to be the right one. Every tribe in Africa speaks its own language."

"But some of the Negroes in town—wouldn't some of them be able to speak?"

"The free Negroes in New Haven speak the language of the country they were born in, same as you and I," Gibbs answered. "Since the days of the Declaration of Independence there hasn't been an African slave brought to Connecticut. But you're right, that's what we've got to have—a native-born African of the same tribe as these people, and one who speaks English, too."

"However could we do that?" Ellis asked.

"If we had some clue to their language, we might look for seamen of their tribe on British ships. We could go down to the water front in Boston—or better still, New York. It's our only chance, and it'll take a miracle to turn up such a man."

As the three white men whispered together, Cinque saw a cloud cross the face of Graham Ellis. He guessed the problem—the old problem of lan-

guage. There was Antonio of course. But after the first thought, Cinque put that name from his mind. Once the masters were in power, Antonio had showed his true colors, caring nothing for truth.

"What did you expect?" he had taunted, when the chains were fastened to Cinque's wrists again. And to every lie Montez and Ruiz had told the soldiers, the cabin boy had nodded in monkeylike agreement. Though Antonio spoke enough of the Mandingo tongue, he would not be of use to them.

Ka-le was watching the white men, too. Suddenly he saw Graham Ellis beckon him. The man called Gibbs held up a finger, and said a word in his own language. But Ka-le shook his head. He could not understand.

Gibbs held up a second finger.

"What does he want to say?" Ka-le could have wept with anxiety to understand.

A third finger was raised. Three fingers were held before his face. Three words, one after the other, were spoken in the white man's language.

Suddenly Ka-le had a thought. He too held up one finger. He spoke the word "one" in Mandingo. A second finger, followed by the word "two."

"By George!" Graham Ellis shouted. "The boy's got the notion! Write down the sounds, Professor Gibbs, I'll do the finger work, up to ten."

11. "It Will Take a Miracle"

YOU said it would take a miracle," Graham Ellis reminded Gibbs on the fourth day that they had trudged the water front in New York without success.

"A miracle, and more time than we've got," Professor Gibbs agreed. "Here it is the first of September and the case comes up for trial on the sixth."

The journey from New Haven had been made as swiftly as possible. But at the water front their speed had ended. Every ship in the harbor was crowded with masts, and half of them seemed to be flying the British Jack. Not all of these, of course, had Negro seamen among their crew. But each one had to be boarded, and permission had to be applied for before Professor Gibbs could ask his questions.

Dozens of freed Africans had been met up with. Yet on the fourth day none had recognized the numbers one to ten in the language of the *Amistad* captives.

One sailor, it is true, thought he recognized the language as Mandingo. But he could not speak it. He was of a different tribe.

"Mandingo," Gibbs repeated wearily. "That gives us a clue at least. That means they are from the Mandi country. At the next ship we'll ask if there are any Mandi aboard."

"And the next, and the next!" said Ellis. "I'm afraid, sir, I've brought you on a wild-goose chase. And if we get their story, it may turn out after all that the Negroes are mutineers and killers."

Professor Gibbs looked at the young man. "Do you believe that?" he asked.

"No," Ellis stammered. "Frankly, I do not. But then I don't believe in slavery. My mother, you see, was a Quaker."

"I have no Quaker tradition," Gibbs answered soberly. "But I have read the Declaration of Independence. That's enough reason to make one want to get rid of slavery." He looked up at the street sign and then at his watch. "I see we're on Pearl Street. That's not far from the Tappan Brother's store. I suggest we go there. Perhaps we can enlist the help of Lewis Tappan or some of his friends to make the rounds of these ships."

Graham Ellis stopped short. "The Tappans are abolitionists!"

"Long-haired men and short-haired women?" Gibbs laughed a little bitterly. "I'm afraid you've been reading the newspapers, Mr. Ellis. I go quite regularly to the barber and I'm a member of the Antislavery Society. There are many of us in New Haven. Young Enoch Hopkins' father has a room in his hayloft where slaves, escaping to freedom, find rest and food for the night."

Ellis was silent a moment. Then he shook his head. "I suppose I hadn't stopped to figure it out. I just took people's word for it—that abolitionists were just—well, queer."

"Sometimes people are called queer when they believe a thing sincerely and try to do something about it, as you are doing now," Gibbs answered. "I think before this case is won you will see a good deal more of the abolitionists and will think differently about them."

"Abolitionist or not," Ellis said, "if Lewis Tappan can help us find an interpreter we'd better go see him."

It was two days later that Lewis Tappan walked with them to a carriage. A young British seaman,

James Covey, climbed to the front seat with the driver. Covey had been born in the Mandi country and captured as a slave seven years ago. But the slave ship in which he was being transported was halted and searched on the high seas by an English cruiser.

The head of the court at Havana, Dr. Madden, had set Covey free, and he had enlisted as a seaman. He was an Englishman now, but he had not forgotten his native tongue.

It was Graham Ellis who had found Covey on the *Buzzard*, a brig just come into port. Tappan had arranged for him to be released from the British service to act as interpreter for the *Amistad* captives.

The abolitionists had also engaged a lawyer, John Staples, to go along to Connecticut to defend the Negroes in court. It was Tappan's own carriage which would take the four men, at full speed, back to New Haven. As Professor Gibbs had said, the abolitionists not only believed that slavery was wrong; they did things about it.

Enoch Hopkins was waiting when the carriage pulled up at the college door.

"We've ridden all night," Ellis said, "with fresh horses waiting for us at Norwalk and Southport. I think we've come as fast as a steam train could carry us."

"I've got a lawyer who'll defend the captives," Enoch said. "It's Mr. Baldwin."

Ellis laughed. "So have we! We brought a lawyer from New York, and we've found an interpreter. Let's get over to the prison right away."

At the prison, the captives had just been given their morning meal. Mr. Pendleton objected to their being disturbed.

"They don't half eat anyhow," he complained, "no matter what my wife fixes 'em. It's a nuisance. I'll be glad when they're turned back to their rightful masters. I'm not used to such a crowd of prisoners, let alone savages. Never had more than three or four people in jail at once before."

All the while the man was grumbling, however, he was leading the way to the cells. Before he opened the door, Ellis asked if Cinque could be brought. The jailer grunted. "I just leave him with the rest of 'em now," he said. "With his chains on, of course. It was my wife's idea. Seems like it makes 'em more contented." Still grumbling, he opened the door.

James Covey stepped inside. After the first glance, the captives hardly looked at him. He was just another stranger. Though his skin was dark, he wore the stiff, heavy clothes of the white men. Then he spoke a few words in the singsong music of the Mandingo language.

This man could speak to them and for them! He was a Mandi like themselves. Everyone began to talk at once, in a transport of joy. When the shouting had died down, James Covey turned to the white men at the door.

"They are Bozals," he said, "captured against the law of nations, as I was. If the slave ship *Tecora*, on which they were first taken to Cuba, had been searched they would have all been set free. They come from my country. The thin one, whose name is Fulway, knows my river, the Saywaye. Also another one, by name of Kimbo, lived near the ancient city of Mali, which was destroyed in my father's time."

Then he turned again to listen to Cinque, who spoke long and seriously.

"He says it is true he killed the captain of that ship," Covey translated. "He bids me say that he alone is responsible. But he would not allow any other killing. The crew, he says, left the ship in safety. And he did what he did because he did not think it was right for Mandi to be slaves."

12. By Wagon and Barge

THEM as are going up to Hartford have got to have decent Christian clothes," Mrs. Pendleton said to her husband. The jail on the Green at New Haven was also the Pendleton home, and Mrs. Pendleton ran it as she would her own household. She wanted the Africans who were going to be taken to the District Court to be a credit to her. "How many are going?" she insisted.

Mr. Pendleton scratched his head and considered. "There's Cinque, of course. He's going to be charged with the murder of Ramon Ferrer, before the Grand Jury. The other leaders of the mutiny will be wanted as witnesses. And there is talk of taking some of the young ones—to melt the hearts of people like you, I wouldn't wonder."

"You heard what Mr. Ellis said," his wife interrupted. "It wasn't mutiny at all for them to take possession of that ship, because they weren't rightly slaves."

Pendleton shrugged impatiently. "The Cubans paid good money for 'em, didn't they? Showed me their papers yesterday when they came up to see why we were holding their property. They want their slaves turned over to 'em. All but Cinque! They're willing for him to be sent to the gallows for murder."

"I don't even know if I'd call Cinque a murderer," Mrs. Pendleton said. "Not the way that interpreter explained it to Mr. Ellis."

"Cinque admits the killing," Pendleton shouted angrily. It was hard enough having all these college professors and lawyers and interpreters fretting about his prisoner. Now if his own wife was going to act as if he was keeping chains on a hero, it was just too much! As if he had any say about it anyway until the courts had spoken!

Mrs. Pendleton smiled and patted her husband's arm. "It's kind of hard on us both," she said, "being pushed into the middle of something the whole town is talking about."

"The town? It's got the whole country excited. You ought to see the New York and Boston papers."

"Anyhow," his wife said soothingly, "you tell me how many are going up the river to Hartford. I'll look around and find 'em some proper shirts and trousers."

Mr. Pendleton had decided to take his charges part way in wagons, part way by river barge. That was the cheapest and safest way to get to Hartford in time for the trials.

The lawyers and Mr. Ellis had gone ahead by coach, the same coach occupied by the Cubans. Lieutenant Commander Gedney had chosen to go alone on horseback. He no longer wanted to be in the presence of the Spanish gentlemen he had rescued.

At first Señor Montez and Señor Ruiz had been full of thanks. They had even put a long notice in the New York papers praising Gedney's noble deed. But when it became clear that the Americans expected salvage money, their gratefulness had melted away.

They blamed the commander of the *Washington* for the delay in the return of the slaves, the ship, and other merchandise on board.

One of the questions to be decided in the court today was whether Gedney had a right to a reward and, if so, how much. Gedney and the Spaniards were equally firm in their claim that the Negroes were part of the property in question. But they differed on whether any "salvage" or reward was due.

"It's only when these rival claims are argued that we can bring forward your story," the lawyers had explained to Cinque and his companions. "We shall say that none of you is property at all, that you are all free men."

James Covey had translated as best he could. Cinque had listened to the interpreter intently. "It is like that under the palaver tree in our villages," Cinque said. "Men declare many things, and then the old men try to sift out the truth."

He was anxious that the truth be known, so his people would get home again. But for himself there was this other trial, for the killing. Cinque knew the white man's law. He had known it in Havana. When he said farewell to the captives left behind in the New Haven prison, it was a long good-by. He did not expect to return; he did not expect to see his wife and son or his planting fields again.

When they climbed into wagons to make the first part of the journey, Ka-le sat next to Cinque, with James Covey on the other side. It was a sunshiny day, a day for singing, but there was no song on the boy's lips. He felt awkward and uncomfortable in long trousers and scratchy shirt, and he felt strange and a little frightened.

Not as frightened as the girls, perhaps, in the other wagon. Marga had cried, and when Mr. Pendleton offered her a red fruit, round like a ball, she had refused to touch it. Ka-le would not be afraid of a strange piece of fruit. But still he felt lost in the harshness and strangeness of this land.

Horses, and not oxen, pulled the wagon along the road. But there were fat, sleek cattle in the fields, worth many a "bride present." The fields rolled by, the green pasture and the brown harvested grain.

Cinque looked at the fields, too, with a farmer's eye. "What are those mounds like small houses, and those others resembling skirted figures in the field?" he asked.

"They are called haystacks and cornstacks," Covey answered. "The dried stalks are used to feed and bed down the cattle when the cold comes and the ground is hard and barren."

He saw the puzzled looks on the part of his listeners. In the Mandi country there is no winter. How could he explain the frozen winter, the ice and snow of the north?

"It rains, but it doesn't rain," he began. "The water from the sky freezes. There is a thing called *snow* that lies on the ground for many moons." Covey could not think of a word for snow in Mandingo. He had used the English word instead.

"Snow?" Cinque repeated.

"Oh, before many moons you'll see what snow looks like." The young seaman laughed, remembering his own first amazed taste of winter. "You'll see so much snow you'll wish you had never heard of it."

"You forget," Cinque answered quietly. He glanced down at the chains on his wrists below the calico shirt sleeves. "I have killed, and I will be killed. I shall not live to see the thing sifting from the sky called *snow*."

But Cinque was mistaken.

Twenty-three men in the courtroom—the Grand Jury—listened to the judge and the District Attorney and the witnesses. Then, while the people waited outside the courtroom door, the Grand Jury discussed the matter of the charge against Cinque.

Suddenly there was a ripple of talk. The charge of murder against Cinque had been dismissed! The American courts, the Grand Jury found, had no

right to try a man for a deed done on the high seas
in a foreign ship.

The chains were taken from Cinque's arms and
legs. Mr. Pendleton led him back into the waiting
room, to a place among the other captives whose
future was at stake.

When Montez saw the chains being taken off the
prisoner, he scowled darkly. These American juries
and foolish American laws!

But Ruiz did not mind. When the slaves were
back in his possession in Havana, Cinque would not
only be hanged, but his body would be drawn and
quartered. His punishment would be an example
to all slaves who rise against their masters.

But it seemed also that in the matter of turning
over his slaves there was going to be some delay.
The court refused to decide at once between Gedney's claim for salvage and the claim of the Spaniards. The judge and witnesses must make a journey back to the very spot where the *Amistad* was
rescued from the hands of the Africans. They must
measure high tide and low tide to decide which
court, that of Connecticut or of the United States,
should settle the claims.

The case was postponed from the sixth to the

nineteenth of September. Then it was postponed again until November.

When at last Judge Judson gave his ruling, Montez and Ruiz could barely contain their anger. The judge had said that the Negroes were not lawfully slaves.

This was not to be tolerated! Ruiz and Montez rushed to the capital at Washington to see the Spanish Ambassador. The lawyers for Cinque had pointed to a treaty. Let the Ambassador find a treaty, too.

The Ambassador called on an important man in the government, on Mr. Forsythe, the Secretary of State.

Mr. Forsythe was very understanding. He was from Georgia, and a friend of Mr. Nicholas Trist in Cuba. He would do all he could to see that the Spanish slaves were returned. Unfortunately, he said, he could not do exactly as the Spaniards wished. It was not permitted him to send an order to the prison in New Haven to turn over the slaves and be done with it. This was not the American way. The case would be taken to a higher court, the Circuit Court. As for the captives, he said, they should be kept in New Haven until it had been decided whether they were slave or free. But he thought he could promise that Señor Ruiz and Señor Montez would have satisfaction in the end.

The Cuban planters sputtered and snorted. They left their case in the care of their Ambassador and boarded a ship for Havana, declaring in loud, shrill tones that they would never set foot on American soil again.

13. In the Time of Snow

THAT is it, the snow!" Again Ka-le stood at the barred window of the room, facing the New Haven Green. Outside, the bare-limbed trees rattled like the rat-tat-tat of drums. But the sound was muffled in a cloud of white, falling feathers.

The window glass had grown suddenly cold to Ka-le's touch. The narrow wooden frames around the glass held mounds of white, like coconut meat. On the iron bars the flakes settled delicately. Ka-le saw that they were not so much like feathers as like fallen stars.

Snow! James Covey had taught Ka-le the word and now he was seeing the mysterious thing itself. At his amazed cry, several of the boys trudged across the room. All of them, even Pugnaw, moved noisily in shoes.

Pugnaw was not content merely to look at the snow. He pushed open the window a crack and stuck his hand out. Starry flakes lit on his palm. Eagerly he closed his fist on them and drew his arm out of the cold. But when he opened his hand, there was nothing to be seen but a few drops of water.

"Snow is to look at. I could not hold it," Pugnaw said sadly, and ran back to watch Fulway carve a ship.

Since the day Fulway had received the gift of a sculptor's knife from Graham Ellis, he had been carving this symbol of the ship that would take them home. In all the pieces of soft wood he gathered for carving, he could see only ships—ships with their prows facing the east! Fulway, the sculptor, carved ships as though they were charms to end this time of waiting, just as Gnakowki made his songs about the land of the sun.

A strange sort of household this prison had become. In the months of waiting for the Americans to decide their fate, the *Amistad* captives were prisoners. Yet within the walls they had not only freedom to move, but work and pleasures. Most of all, they had the pleasure of friendship. They had learned enough of the language of the white men and of their ways to feel unafraid.

They had even learned to eat the strange foods, especially after Fulway discovered that corn oil could be used like the oil of the palm. Mrs. Pendleton had given over the cooking to Fulway, as she had given over much of the sewing and mending and weaving to the girls. The cheap cloth to clothe the prisoners was bought, though Mrs. Pendleton herself had never discarded her loom. The African girls were skilled at using a loom.

At first, wearing white men's clothes had seemed a great trial. As the cold weather came on, however, even the heavy shoes for the feet had been welcomed. Shoes made walking clumsy, but they were needed in this climate; and the clothes, even if awkwardly made and unbeautiful, were warm.

Best of all was the teaching. Every day someone, Professor Gibbs or Graham Ellis or Enoch, or some of their friends, came across the Green from the college. They taught the white man's language, and they taught those who wished to learn, first how to read the alphabet and then words from a printed page.

When Ka-le first came to understand that certain marks on a page were symbols of his name, he strutted about like a young tiger. He would search for a *K* or an *L* or *E* as eagerly as he used to look for omens on his morning walks in the village. Finally he knew all the symbols for that thing

Enoch called *the alphabet*. He could pick out Marga's name and Cinque's, and the names for sun and moon, and for animals. He knew the alphabet. He could read! It was a great wonder.

Reading was hard work for the older men. They muttered to themselves quite loudly as they read. Big drops of sweat stood on their brows. But for Ka-le, reading seemed to come easily. Even Cinque could not read any better than Ka-le.

He had three books of his own that Graham Ellis had brought him: a spelling book with a blue cover, a book of stories about the God of the white men, and a book that had amusing pictures. Even its name, *Mother Goose*, was funny. And the words were singing words; they had a pleasant flow, like songs in Mandingo.

Mr. Ellis had said the books were Ka-le's own, no matter what happened! There was a troubled look on his face when he said, "No matter what. . . ." Ka-le thought of those words now as he stood at the window watching the silent fall of snow.

Until the time of snow nothing would be decided, James Covey had explained two moons ago. He had gone off to his ship; but now he was back, and the deciding—the court trial—had begun again.

There had been no teaching today or yesterday because of the trial. Cinque and Grabeau had gone off with Mr. Pendleton early in the morning. Mr. Staples and Mr. Baldwin had gone with them. They were the lawyers who would palaver with the wise man, the judge, in the court. It was hard to understand what was going on, even when James Covey explained in Mandingo. So much of the talk at Court seemed to concern other things than the question of their freedom.

As the first surprise of the snow began to fade, Ka-le's thoughts turned more and more anxiously toward the happenings in the court.

There had been rumor of a ship in the harbor—not a good ship—to carry them home again. Instead, it was a ship to take them back to Havana. What if the judge decided that they were slaves and the property of the Spaniards? What if he said they must go on that ship?

Ka-le shivered and pressed his hands against the cold, barred window. It is not right for Mandi to be slaves, Cinque had said. His mother also had said it when she gave him the file as a farewell gift. His mother, who was not in the land of the living!

Ka-le knew this to be so because a man had come from Havana, a good man, Dr. Madden. Before

coming to America as a witness he had gone to the
barracoon and talked with the slave dealer's attendant. This man had told the true story of the stay in
the barracoon. When he heard how Cinque had
sailed the ship but had after all not come to his
home, he had said, "What a pity!"

Dr. Madden had told these things, and now he
was at the trial with Cinque and Grabeau. Would
the judge listen?

Ka-le's hand felt cold on the window. His heart,
too, was cold within him. He sighed, thinking of
that dreadful ship in the harbor.

Marga came up behind him. He heard her laugh
before he felt the touch of her fingers on his sleeve.
He whirled around and saw that she held something in her other hand, hidden in the folds of her
skirt.

A surprise again! Ka-le chuckled. Marga was always full of surprises. An apple? A sweet cake she
had baked? A handful of nuts?

Marga's surprise was none of these. It was large
and white. She held it out in both hands, a great
square piece of cloth.

"It's finished!" Her eyes were bright. "Mrs. Pendleton helped me take it off the loom but the weaving is mine, all mine."

"What is it?" Ka-le asked.

"A sail for your river boat," Marga's voice was suddenly shy. "You said when you get home you want a sail, so you can go faster than any boys in your village."

When you get home! Marga was not worried about this trial. But then she had not listened to the talk as he had. She had been busy weaving. Ka-le took the sail with hands that trembled. Perhaps it was an omen. "Go ye ahead upon the way, tell them we are coming, like bright lizards running."

Outside it was dark, but not quite dark because of the snow that glowed from lighted candles in the windows of the houses around the Green. Muffled footsteps sounded outside the house. Mrs. Pendleton could be heard lifting the chain off the door. Then there was a great clatter of tramping feet, and the sound of voices and laughter.

Crowds followed Cinque and Grabeau into the hallway and flowed through the open doors of the rooms. A look at Cinque's face was enough for Ka-le to know that the news was good.

"The judge has spoken. We are free!" The rest of Cinque's words were drowned in a clamor of joyous shouts.

Free! That word of Tua's! Tua had not been mistaken.

That night had been the happiest that Ka-le could remember. On the morrow the happiness melted like snowflakes in Pugnaw's hand. Mr. Forsythe and Mr. Holabird, the District Attorney, had ordered an appeal.

Graham Ellis sat at a table with Cinque, trying to explain. "The ruling seemed so just, so fair, we didn't think there'd be any more to it. The Circuit Court judge allowed a reward to Gedney for salvaging the ship and cargo for the Spanish owners. He decreed that Antonio, the cabin boy, the Ladino, was to go back to Cuba as slave to the wife of Ramon Ferrer. Seems that's what the boy wants, or thinks he wants."

Cinque sat in the stiff chair of a white man and stared straight ahead. He thought of the wretched, lying boy. How could it be that even such a one would choose slavery? Is this what happens when one has not known freedom?

But no, that is not so. Cinque had seen with his own eyes a woman, born a slave, from a place far off to the south. This woman had walked a thousand miles in twenty nights, following a star, in order to be free. Cinque had talked to her briefly one

day when he went to the Hopkins farm for a visit. From her he had learned that a slave longs all through life for freedom.

Cinque spread out his hands, palms up, as if to say that Antonio's miserable choice was a thing he could not grasp.

"The case of Antonio is finished," Ellis declared. "It is the part of the ruling that concerns you and your people that will be considered again in the highest court. This is the meaning of the appeal."

"Then the waiting is not over," Cinque studied the troubled eyes of the man sitting opposite him. "They have reasons?"

Graham Ellis scowled. "The same old reasons," he answered. "The reasons that people who enslave others can always find. The Spanish Ambassador claims that the vessel, cargo, and property rescued out of the hands of robbers and pirates shall be restored to the owners. He points to a treaty."

"But Mr. Baldwin has said we are not pirates!" Cinque answered. "Pirates are violent men. It is true I was forced to kill the captain of the *Amistad*, but the lives of those others were spared."

"We have said that you are not pirates; that the only pirates are those that kidnaped you and put you into the hands of Ruiz and Montez. We have said that human beings are not property; that the Spaniards are not your owners. We have said that the passports which name you as Ladinos, when you are really Bozals, are a fraud and a lie. We shall have to say these things again."

Cinque followed the words with careful attention. When Ellis had ceased speaking, he leaned forward. "I have not tried before to speak what was in my heart," he said. "I have been moved many times to speak, but the language escapes me. That *we* should defend our own freedom is natural. But that all of you have done this thing for strangers in an alien country—"

Ellis interrupted. "It's not for you alone, it is for ourselves too that we need to act for the sacred promise on which America is founded. While some men are enslaved, we believe that none is truly free."

He paused, wondering if he could make his meaning clear to Cinque. "One of our great men put it this way: 'We hold these truths to be self-evident, that all men are created equal; that they are endowed by their creator with certain unalienable rights; that among these are life, liberty, and the pursuit of happiness.' If the Declaration of Independence isn't for everybody it hasn't any meaning at all!"

Life, liberty, and happiness. Cinque turned the words over his mind, in his own language: to live, to be free, to know the happiness of putting his hand to his plow, to plow his field with his son beside him . . . "It is a good promise," he said. "I will explain to the others. They will understand. We will wait in patience."

The troubled look left Graham Ellis' eyes. "There is another thing," he said. "The Supreme Court to which the case will be carried is very important. The Attorney General will place his arguments before it. Mr. Baldwin thinks that you too should have an important man to speak. There is such a man, one who was President when I was a boy no older than Pugnaw. His name is John Quincy Adams."

"Adams," Cinque repeated the name carefully. It was another word he must learn.

"After he ceased to be President of the United States," Ellis continued, "Adams went back into the government as a lawmaker from his own state of Massachusetts. In the spring, he is to be in the city of New York. I have permission to take you and such others as you choose to meet John Quincy Adams. He is an old man now and goes rarely to the courts, but it may be that he will speak for your freedom."

"And Mr. Baldwin?" Cinque asked.

"He too will make an argument. But he is a man like I am—neither important nor famous."

Cinque smiled. "You are my friends. When we get home, your names will be famous in the Mandi country."

14. An Old Man Changes His Mind

WHAT I can't understand is, if you don't have winter, how do you know when it's time for spring cleaning?" Mrs. Pendleton looked from one girl to the other as she shook sand on the kitchen floor to get ready for scrubbing.

Ferni laughed. She had no words to explain that you couldn't scrub a cookhouse floor in her village, since the floor was made of hard-packed earth. You couldn't wash windows if you didn't have any glass in the openings. Where the days are warm and the nights pleasant, there is no need to shut in a window with glass.

You didn't dust pictures of flowers hanging on a wall in a Mandi village. You picked fresh flowers and stuck them in your hair or made ropes of flowers over your doorway. But all this was too hard to explain. It would be equally impossible to tell the women in the village at home about the American ways. When the trials were over, that is, and a ship took them back to their own land.

For there was to be such a ship! The court, called the Circuit Court, had decreed it. To be sure, in their strange way of going from one court to another the Americans had "appealed" again. Cinque had explained this, and then had gone off in a carriage with the white men to another city. He had taken Fulway and Kimbo and Ka-le.

Grabeau would have gone, too, if he had not been working for that blacksmith. Since he had been allowed to work at the forge, Grabeau went off every morning with a song on his lips like a singing man. He said it was more important to mend plows for the farmers than to go to meet the man who had been a Paramount Chief.

The truth was that Grabeau, since he had begun working with the iron he loved, had ceased to think as the others did of the ship that would take them home. If the high court decreed that they were free to choose, Grabeau would stay in America, to work at the forge and help other slaves to freedom.

Ferni glanced at Teme, with her head wrapped up in a cloth, sweeping the cobwebs from above the cookstove. Teme had become a woman, and it had been decided that she was to be given in marriage to Bau. They would be married when Cinque came back again, in the church across the Green.

Would Teme and Bau choose to stay in this strange land too? Would Teme someday be sweeping cobwebs from her own chimney? Ferni started to ask, but then a sad thought came to her. Suppose Teme and Bau, with the rest of them, were sent to Cuba, to slavery again? It was better to wait, and not to dream until that court they called the Supreme Court had spoken.

Meanwhile the waiting was not a bad time, especially now that the bitter cold and the snow were gone and the world was turning green. Ferni picked up the scrub brush and got down on her knees as she saw Mrs. Pendleton doing. She laughed again. It would be a thing worth telling about at home, this spring cleaning!

April 19, 1840. John Quincy Adams read no more than the date on the newspaper. Then he folded it back in his pocket and began restlessly pacing the floor of his hotel room. The date was sixty-six years, to the day, from the Battle of Lexington, where the United States of America might rightly be said to have begun!

He'd been a boy, eight years old, when the first musket shot for independence was fired. A serious-minded boy, growing up in a family deep in the struggle for freedom. And at the close of the war, he'd been old enough, in his father's eyes at least, to be present in Paris when the treaty of peace was signed.

Harvard College had followed, and a few years—the years when his father was President—had been occupied in the practice of law. Then had come a new battleground, the glittering courts of Moscow, of London, of the Paris of Napoleon's empire. The battle here was to make the rest of the world respect the young republic. It had not been easy to win respect for a republic in the courts of emperors.

Again a shift of battleground, to the half-finished capital built on the Potomac. In the Senate, and as adviser of two Presidents. Then the battle for the Presidency itself. When the four years in high office were over, a man might have expected the years of struggle to be over.

Instead had come a shift of battleground again: back to the lawmaking body, the House of Representatives. Here to fight the long discouraging battle for justice to the Indians, to the neighboring country of Mexico. And, most pressing of all, the fight to allow the slaves to petition against slavery. "We who are not slave owners are told to mind our own business; but to dislike and to oppose slavery is the business of the free men." The battle for the right of petition was not yet won.

Through the long years there had been the struggle to make worth while those musket shots heard sixty-six years ago on the road to Lexington. Now, after so many years of fighting, on so many battlefields, a new battleground was offering itself. There was this request to defend the *Amistad* captives in the Supreme Court battle.

"It's thirty years since I've been in a law court," the old man said to himself. "It's too late to shift battlegrounds again. I'll see this Cinque when he comes, but I'll tell him to find another lawyer to speak for him."

His mind made up, Adams pulled out his paper, the *Log Cabin.* He unfolded the thin little sheet that sold for a penny. It didn't look like much; but the editor, young Horace Greeley, had a lively way of writing and of finding the important news.

It was Greeley who'd requested him to take the *Amistad* case. He was sorry to disappoint the fiery little editor. But it was asking too much of a man of seventy-two to speak up in a new struggle.

Adams had hardly begun to read when a tap on the door brought him to his feet. Cinque stood on the threshold.

There were others with him: a tall, lean Negro, a younger one with a flower in his buttonhole, and a half-grown boy. There were several white men, too. But John Quincy Adams saw them only as statues filling the background. He looked up into the eyes of the young African farmer who had, quite simply, refused to accept the role of slave, for himself or for others.

The old man, who had been President of the United States, had often found himself in the presence of great men. He had known most of the leaders of his time in his own country and in Europe. He could recognize the spark of greatness when he saw it. It was visible now in the remarkable eyes, in the poise, in the smile of the young Negro in badly fitting clothes, who stood waiting.

"We have come, sir," Cinque said, in slow, careful English.

Adams held out his hand, and Cinque took it in his own, in white-man fashion. Adams forgot that he was old, forgot that he had fought too many battles to begin another. He motioned the company to chairs and sat down, facing Cinque.

"Now tell me," he said, "just how you think I can help."

15. Enoch Asks a Question

IN back of the Hopkins farm there was a little stream, hardly more than a pond, fed by "runs" from the hills. Here the cattle came to drink. Here, too, Enoch kept a homemade boat, moored to a birch tree.

The quiet water was overhung with trees: one huge maple, and some birches and dogwoods. With the first frost, the trees had turned. But before the winds came to strip them of their leaves, the weather had grown warm again. The red and copper of the leaves were mirrored in the water. Their beauty was not a thing that could be described in any language.

Ka-le stood on the bank with Enoch, speechless with wonder.

"Pretty, isn't it?" Enoch said, with the understatement common to New Englanders. "Just wait till the moon comes up—it'll take your breath away.

Come on out in my boat. We'll go upstream to meet the moonrise."

"Your father can spare us from the corn shucking?" Ka-le asked, as Enoch unlooped the rope and loosed the boat from its mooring.

"Sure!" Enoch laughed. "Pa never had so many hands helping on the farm in his life as he's had this summer. Ever since Mr. Pendleton said Cinque and the rest of you could come farming if you wanted to, Pa's fair spoiled. Don't know how he's going to manage when you folks leave."

After Cinque had come back from New York in April, there'd been nothing for the prisoners to do but sit and wait for the Supreme Court to meet in October. When spring came in earnest and the corn started stirring in the ground, Cinque had wandered back and forth restlessly in the Pendleton yard. He had ceased to take an interest in the lessons, ceased to eat, had grown silent and moody.

"There's nothing wrong with Cinque that getting his fingers in the dirt won't cure," Mr. Pendleton had said. "He's a farmer. Come planting time, a farmer just naturally wants to plant."

Next day, the jailer had driven Cinque and a wagonload of his other prisoners out to the Hopkins farm. He had announced to Mr. Hopkins that there was some hired help if there was any work to do.

After that day, the time of waiting for the court ruling had gone by like a breeze in the trees. The captives had weeded and pulled stumps. They had cleared stones for a new field and piled the stones into long walls on the upland meadows. They had helped cut the hay and gather the corn. They had used all their skill as farmers on this alien land.

Now the harvest was over, all but the corn shucking. October was half gone, and the Justices of the Supreme Court were meeting in Washington. Indian summer was putting an end to the time of waiting.

Darkness came abruptly after sunset, and the full harvest moon came up over the trees like a lantern. The two boys had been rowing in silence, each occupied with his own thoughts. Suddenly Enoch rested his oars.

"Do you realize," he asked, "that you've been in America more than a year?"

"Fourteen moons," Ka-le said. "I just counted. I was thinking: where will I see the next moon?"

"Why not here?" Enoch urged. He'd talked it

over with his father, this idea of getting Ka-le to stay.

"You forget, Enoch, the future is not of my choosing."

Enoch's lips tightened. He had to admit that the ruling of the Supreme Court, when their case came up, was by no means certain to go in favor of the *Amistad* captives.

Graham Ellis had gone down to Washington to talk with Mr. Adams. The tutor had come back to Yale plainly discouraged. He had hidden his anxiety from the prisoners, but at the college he had spoken of the many forces working against a favorable decision.

There was Spain for one thing. The Spanish Ambassador insisted that the Africans were a lot of rebellious slaves and mutineers who should be turned over without more delay. The señores had paid good money for them. The Secretary of State and the Attorney General wanted to please the Ambassador from Spain. They said it was the duty of the United States to return the slaves to their owners.

There was also another reason in the back of some minds. Many men in the government, from the southern states, were slaveholders themselves. They said that if Cinque and his companions

gained their freedom by violent action, other rebellious slaves might follow their example. It was
better to send the captives back to Cuba, to let the
Cubans decide whether they were slaves or free
men.

It was not the business of Americans, these slaveholders said, to look for fraud; to say who were
Ladinos, who Bozals.

But John Quincy Adams intended to argue that
it was not the business of the United States Government to enslave! And Mr. Baldwin was busy, too,
marshaling the facts that had convinced two lower
courts that the Negroes were not the lawful property of Montez and Ruiz.

There had been only one difference between the
rulings of the District and Circuit Courts. The
District Court had declared that the Negroes were
free to go home or to stay in America if they
pleased. The Circuit Court had ordered them all
sent home to Africa.

As the boat drifted in the moonlight, Enoch real-
ized that Ka-le was right. Even if the Supreme
Court decided favorably in their case, the Negroes
might not have the choice of going home or remaining in America.

To Cinque and to most of the others, one ruling

would seem the same as another. Cinque had but a single object: to return to his home, his land, his family. If the United States Government was ordered to provide a ship, well and good. If the judges declared him free to choose where he would live, the first ship that sailed for Africa would find Cinque aboard.

There'd be no trouble about money for the passage; Cinque had earned that. For those of his companions who had not the means to pay, money would be forthcoming from the Antislavery Society, from Lewis Tappan, and from Professor Gibbs.

But not all of the Africans would return home if a choice were given them. Grabeau had said that he would stay at the blacksmith shop; and Teme and Bau, since their marriage in the church, wanted to become Americans. Enoch hoped that Ka-le would be among those who would decide to remain in America.

"If you could choose, Ka-le," he asked, "would you stay here? You could live with us. My parents are willing. You could work at a trade as Grabeau plans to do, or on our farm or in town, the way Bau is going to work for Mr. Pendleton. Or you could go to school and maybe even to college."

A look of surprise crossed Ka-le's face. He had

met many free Negroes living in New Haven, but none of them was a scholar at Yale.

"Negroes haven't had as good a chance as other folk in the United States," Enoch said. "But they will someday. I'm bound they will. If you stayed, Ka-le, it might be that you could go to Yale."

Ka-le watched the ripples in the water as the boat drifted in the path of the moonlight. To go to school . . . to read more books than the books Graham Ellis had given him! Ka-le sucked in his breath with pleasure at the thought.

But life in his own village, that was good too. To get up when the sun rises and race down to the river, to lead the cattle out, to climb palm trees! The palms did not turn gold and red with the seasons, but they gave food and oil and bark for man's use.

If he went home, he could try out Marga's sail and see his boat skim along the river. He could sit under the palaver tree and tell the story of his mother's gift of the file, and how it had helped save many people from slavery. Ka-le looked at his friend. "I don't know, Enoch," he said. "It will be a hard choosing."

Enoch did not answer. He took up the oars abruptly and sent the boat skimming toward the shore.

16. The End of a Voyage

IN Washington on a blustery evening in March 1841, in a long narrow room over a barbershop, eight men sat around a table. They were the Justices of the Supreme Court, meeting together to decide and give a ruling on the case of the *Amistad*.

Justice Story of Massachusetts had been chosen to write the decision. After the other judges had heard Story's decision they would add their names to his, if they agreed. If they did not, they would dissent. The decision agreed on by the majority would stand as the ruling of the Court. Once agreed on, the decree would be handed down from the bench in open court, with the eight judges soberly robed in black robes.

But tonight they were meeting without ceremony to try to get the business over. It had already gone on too long. The Court Calendar had been crowded with cases. The October term of the Court had lasted through the fall and winter.

The new year had come in, and a new President had entered the White House. The Inauguration ceremonies had broken into the work of the Court. There had been special duties to perform. Chief Justice Taney had been called on to hear President Harrison, old "Tippecanoe," take his oath of office.

There had been balls and parties to attend. A whole week of March had been taken up with the Inauguration of Harrison and Tyler, while the fate of the *Amistad* captives remained undecided.

Earlier, while the trial was in progress, there had been another delay, caused by the death of one of the judges. There should have been nine men sitting around the table tonight. But Justice Barbour of Virginia had died during the week that John Quincy Adams was arguing before the Court. The trial had been put off for a week. Then Mr. Adams had taken up his argument again before the eight remaining judges.

Now the long arguments for both sides were finished. The Justices had read and examined the evidence. They were familiar with the facts, but they listened carefully while Justice Story restated them.

Justice Story read in his dry voice, reviewing the claims of Lieutenant Gedney, who had taken possession of the vessel, and of the Negroes who had gone on shore. He read the demands of Ruiz and Montez, and of the Spanish Ambassador, that the ship and its cargo should be restored, according to treaty. He outlined the answer of the Negroes.

One hour passed, and then another before Justice Story came to the main points which would be necessary to decide. "The only point is whether these Negroes are the property of Ruiz and Montez, and ought to be delivered up."

Up to this moment his listeners had heard nothing new. Justice Story was coming now to his own decision. The other seven judges stirred and leaned forward in their chairs.

"It is plain," Justice Story said, "that these Negroes were never the lawful slaves of Ruiz or Montez, or of any other Spanish subjects. By the laws of Spain, the African slave trade is abolished; the dealing in that trade is deemed a crime. They cannot be deemed pirates in the sense of the treaty."

The Justice then went on to give his opinion that the passports offered as evidence of ownership had been obtained by fraud. "In the treaties between nations, it can never be presumed that either state intends to protect fraud. When the *Amistad* arrived, she was in possession of the Negroes asserting their freedom. In no sense could they intend to import themselves as slaves. Therefore it is our opinion that the said Negroes be declared free."

When Justice Story finished reading, his eyes fastened themselves on Chief Justice Taney. Would he agree? Would the opinion stand? Taney had only one vote, of course, but his word would have great weight. Taney, like the majority of the men at the table, came from a part of the country where slavery was the law and the custom. He believed there was no wrong in slavery.

"I am in agreement," Taney asserted without hesitation. Five other men nodded. Only Baldwin of Pennsylvania dissented. Seven to one! A clear majority. The fate of the *Amistad* captives was decided.

The men stood up and stretched tired muscles, wearily. The last case on the Court Calendar was closed! The October term at last could come to an end.

The April sun beat heavily on the tropical waters and on the white-sailed brig, the *Buzzard*. But the passengers aboard did not mind the heat of the sun at the Equator. For most of them, it meant that they were nearing home.

An omen, Cinque had called it, that the news from Washington reached the prison at the same time the *Buzzard* was set to sail to Africa. James Covey had spent his shore leave in New Haven and was about to return to his ship when the word of the Supreme Court decree arrived. It was he who had suggested that Captain Fitzgerald's brig could provide transport for the returning Africans.

A church mission had already engaged passage, Captain Fitzgerald said. But he didn't mind crowding his ship a bit for the honor of carrying the *Amistad* captives home. He claimed part of the credit for their freedom anyway. If he had not let his seaman, James Covey, go to New Haven to act as interpreter, Americans might never have known the *Amistad* story.

It had been a good voyage. After only four weeks out, they were already nearing the tropical coastal waters of Africa. Ka-le stood by the rail watching Covey take a reef in the topsail.

The seaman laughed at the sight of Pugnaw climbing the rigging up to the lookout. "Can't keep that one off the ropes," he said. "He's going to make a sailor!"

A sailor! Ka-le's heart missed a beat. As the voyage neared its end, he had blown hot and cold about his decision to return home. When he had told Enoch Hopkins that he was leaving with the others, Enoch had said, moodily, "I knew that night on the pond. If Indian summer on our farm couldn't win you, nothing else would have a chance."

As a matter of fact, Ka-le had been very close to staying in America, until Cinque gave him the file that had brought their freedom. "To remember by," Cinque had said. That file, Ka-le knew, must be taken home to the village.

Then, when Graham Ellis decided to make the voyage with them to Africa, to set up a school in the church mission, Ka-le had no more doubts about his choice.

He wanted to go home, surely. But afterward . . . beyond this year, beyond the next?

Ka-le chuckled. He was thinking like an American. In his village at home, boys did not plan years ahead. They did not consider a future different from that of their fathers or grandfathers. In a way of life set by long tradition, the future took care of itself without special planning.

You grew to manhood and married. You farmed, like Cinque, or raised cattle, or worked in iron or wood, like Grabeau and Fulway. When you were old, you joined the wise men under the palaver tree. Where things happened always in the same way, there was no need to consider your role in the years ahead.

The Americans had a different way. They did

one thing and then another. They tried to know many different kinds of life, in many places.

"How do you get to be a sailor?" Ka-le asked James Covey next time he saw him.

"You just sign up," Covey said. "Getting on the roll is easy. Not so easy to quit the sea. Even if the work below decks is hard, it kind of gets in your blood. Are you thinking of signing? I thought all of you folks were longing to get back to your homes."

To the Negro seaman, it had meant more than he could say to have had a share in the struggle for the freedom these Africans had waged. Not he alone, but all Negroes everywhere who had been torn from their homes by white invaders had had their spirits uplifted by the triumph of the *Amistad* captives. "It's a great thing you've accomplished, getting back," Covey said in a low, serious tone.

"I know," Ka-le responded. "But the world is big. I want to see all of it. Not right away, but in the future."

To go home, to tell all the happenings, to have Marga's parents come perhaps to bargain for a wedding. But someday, before he was an old man, to handle ropes and sail at sea . . . A great clamor woke Ka-le out of his daydream.

"Land, ho!" the lookout shouted.

From the deck on which he was standing, the coast seemed no more than a dark line drawn against the sky with a pen. Marga came to stand beside the rail. She did not speak, but just stood there straining her eyes to see the shore.

Presently she pulled Ka-le's sleeves and whispered, "Look." She pointed to the helm. Cinque was at the wheel. He was guiding the ship with Captain Fitzgerald standing beside him!

Graham Ellis came up with one of the ladies of the mission. "Did you see Cinque at the helm?" the lady asked. "Mr. Ellis suggested it and Captain Fitzgerald thought it very fitting."

Ka-le nodded. He could not trust himself to speak. To see Cinque with his hand on the wheel, brought back the long, fruitless days on the black schooner, the *Amistad*. The days of toilsome journeying that were so cruelly undone in the night! Yet the toil, the hunger and thirst, the sickness, the dying, had not been in vain.

The faint pencil-mark strip of land became a definite shore line, with earth and palm trees. Ahead lay the Lomboko harbor. Cinque had brought the voyagers home.